Mastering Uncertainty

Praise for *Mastering Uncertainty*

'With verve and wit, *Mastering Uncertainty* explores the psychological and practical aspects of confronting and ultimately prevailing over the unpredictable forces that shape the business landscape.'

Geoff Lewis, founder and Managing Partner, Bedrock Capital

'*Mastering Uncertainty* is a great book. It will teach you to stop searching for definitive answers that don't exist, and embrace a world of possibilities and probabilities. Along the way you'll discover opportunities that you were blind to before, and how to turn more of them into positive outcomes.'

Jim O'Shaughnessy, *New York Times* bestselling author of *Invest Like the Best, What Works on Wall Stree*t and *Predicting the Markets of Tomorrow* and Chairman and Co-Chief Investment Officer of O'Shaughnessy Asset Management (OSAM)

'Finally, a business book that explains how to succeed out there in the messy, real world. *Mastering Uncertainty* is essential reading.'

Charlene Li, *New York Times* bestselling author of *The Disruption Mindset* and founder of Altimeter

'Compelling, entertaining, and actionable, *Mastering Uncertainty* is an incredible distillation of methods and mentalities to help you succeed whatever the future brings.'

Jeremy M. Isaacs CBE, founding partner at JRJ Group, former CEO, Lehman Brothers

'Embracing uncertainty is at the core of the entrepreneurial spirit. This vital book explains how to adopt such a mindset and successfully apply it to a vast range of personal and professional scenarios. A wonderful read.'

Steve Tidball, CEO and founder, Vollebak

'Managing uncertainty is the key leadership skill. Thriving in an unpredictable world is possible, and it is the vital lessons from *Mastering Uncertainty* that can help you succeed.'

Joanna Maryewska, General Manager and founder, SAP.iO Venture Studio

'Beautifully written and eminently practical, *Mastering Uncertainty* is a treasure trove of valuable life and business advice.'

Peter Bauer, CEO, Mimecast

'*Mastering Uncertainty* is a practical guide to probabilistic decision-making in business as well as life. It will help you understand the differences between successful entrepreneurs and ineffective traditional managers, and why it is critical to think in terms of acceptable loss, not probable gain.'

Jack Schwager, author of the *Market Wizards* series, Chief Research Officer at FundSeeder Technologies

'Every chapter of *Mastering Uncertainty* is packed with practical advice for how to succeed in our unpredictable world.'

Steven Drobny, CEO of Clocktower Group, author of *Inside The House of Money* and *The Invisible Hands*

'*Mastering Uncertainty* is the "red pill" of business books. It will fundamentally change your understanding of how the world works, and radically improve your odds of success in the process.'

Sam Englebardt, General Partner at Galaxy Interactive

'In a thought-provoking collaboration that is a delight to explore, Konkoly and Watkinson provide a practical roadmap to embracing chance and serendipity as a real superpower to thrive in a future where uncertainty is sure to be a feature not to be feared.'

Paul Bricault, Managing Partner, Amplify, and Adjunct Professor, Graduate School of Cinema Arts at USC

'*Mastering Uncertainty* is everything you could want in a business book. It's concise, easy to read, and brimming with practical advice that can elevate your performance.'

Matthew D. Lieberman, PhD, Director, UCLA Social Cognitive Neuroscience Laboratory, and founder of Resonance Inc.

'*Mastering Uncertainty* replaces fear of the unknown, the unpredictable, and the uncontrollable with a feeling of empowerment, and a sense of greater opportunity. It makes you think about taking uncertainty into account, but not letting it keep you from acting. A masterpiece.'

Howard Morgan, Chairman, B Capital Group

'Concise, easy to read, and full of advantageous advice, *Mastering Uncertainty* delivers in spades.'

Tal Barnoach, General Partner at Disruptive VC
and Disruptive AI Venture Capital

'*Mastering Uncertainty* offers a direct shortcut to essential business and life lessons that most take years to learn the hard way.'

Michael Yanover, Head of Business Development, CAA

'*Mastering Uncertainty* carries a profoundly important message about the role of chance events in our successes and failures. A remarkable book.'

Isabel Fox, General Partner, Outsized VC

'If fear of failure, analysis paralysis, or perfectionism are holding you back, *Mastering Uncertainty* is the book you've been waiting for. Stop what you're doing and read it immediately.'

Chris Webb, CEO at ChowNow

'Without uncertainty, there wouldn't be opportunity. The best entrepreneurs use uncertainty to their advantage. If you want to learn how, then you can start by reading this book. You may be pleasantly surprised how a simple shift in mindset can be transformative.'

B. Paul Santos, Managing Partner at Wavemaker Partners

'If you're starting out on your entrepreneurial journey, put *Mastering Uncertainty* to the top of your reading list.'

Mark Lynn, CEO, Amass

'Matt and Csaba have written a remarkably thoughtful and highly personal book. Their insights provide a framework for balancing and, more importantly, taking ownership of the uncertainty that we all live with in our professional and personal lives. I highly recommend it.'

Eric N. Vincent, President, Sarissa Capital,
former Chairman, Managed Funds Association

'With evocative storytelling, *Mastering Uncertainty* provides tools for embracing uncertainty and failure, and multiplying and harnessing moments of leverage.'

Benjamin Katz, serial entrepreneur, founder of
Card.com and current CEO of HappyHead.com

'If you want to create more opportunities for yourself, and convert more of them into outcomes, start by reading *Mastering Uncertainty*.'

Yida Gao, General Partner, Shima Capital, Forbes 30 under 30

'Reading *Mastering Uncertainty* will give you an immediate advantage over the competition. I highly recommend it!'

Sam Shaffer, former Director of Business Development
at Afterpay and eBay

Mastering Uncertainty

*How Great Founders,
Entrepreneurs and Business Leaders
Thrive in an Unpredictable World*

Matt Watkinson
and Csaba Konkoly

Cornerstone Press

1 3 5 7 9 10 8 6 4 2

Cornerstone Press
20 Vauxhall Bridge Road
London SW1V 2SA

Cornerstone Press is part of the Penguin Random House group of companies
whose addresses can be found at global.penguinrandomhouse.com.

Penguin
Random House
UK

First published in the UK by Cornerstone Press in 2023

www.penguin.co.uk

A CIP catalogue record for this book is available from the British Library.

ISBN 9781847943415 (hardback)
ISBN 9781847943422 (trade paperback)

Set in 12.25/16 pt Minion Pro Typeset by Jouve (UK), Milton Keynes
Printed and bound in Great Britain by Clays Ltd, Elcograf S.p.A.

The authorised representative in the EEA is Penguin Random House Ireland,
Morrison Chambers, 32 Nassau Street, Dublin D02 YH68

Penguin Random House is committed to a sustainable future for
our business, our readers and our planet. This book is made from
Forest Stewardship Council® certified paper.

For Marlowe – M.W.

For Sara, Lily, Aaron and Judy – C.K.

Contents

Acknowledgements

We would like to thank the following for their help and support: Louise Watkinson, John Watkinson, Judy Konkoly, Megan Butler, Patrick Walsh, Nigel Wilcockson, Robert van Ossenbruggen, Ben Supper, Matt Neal, Luke Williams, Michelle Carr, Rob Isaacs, Keith Ferrazzi, Robert Kirubi, Linda Schulze, Tamar Cohen, Natalie Malevsky, Cathy Tabatabaie, Chris Duffy, Stephanie Todd and Scott King.

Special thanks to Ben Smith, the best friend and business partner anyone could ask for – M.W.

Introduction

Childhood memories are funny things. I can remember starring as a hedge in the school play when I was little – standing at the back, occasionally rustling my tissue-paper leaves for dramatic effect – but don't remember tumbling down the stairs and breaking my arm, which happened around the same time. I have a grainy photo of another childhood scene on my desk: my brother and I dressed as astronauts, grinning like idiots with our rain boots wrapped in tinfoil. I don't remember this either, but I wish I did. It looks as though we're having the time of our lives.

Memories from my teenage years are also patchy, but I remember a conversation with my father as if it happened yesterday. An engineer by training, Dad was technical director of a company that made loudspeakers for recording studios. As he demonstrated a prototype, I asked how he'd arrived at the design and his response left an indelible impression: 'You start with how the ears work.'

Mastering first principles was crucial when it came to design and engineering, he explained, and applying them rather than copying what already existed was the gateway to innovation. It was reassuring to know that there was an underlying logic to the world, but also exciting. With these invisible laws at our command, I had the sense that anything was possible, a world-view I carried into adulthood.

I began my career designing websites and software. Then, as the number of channels proliferated – apps, kiosks and social media platforms alongside showrooms and contact centres – I found myself helping clients connect them to create complete customer experiences. I studied my field thoroughly, but felt that something was missing from the literature – a set of first principles that were easy to grasp and apply to increase our odds of success.

I set out to fill this important gap myself, and it led to my first book, *The Ten Principles Behind Great Customer Experiences*. It won the CMI's Management Book of the Year, some companies ordered a thousand copies at a time, and I've heard from readers worldwide who have used these simple principles successfully. I was, however, unprepared for the impact on my career. Rather than being asked to do the job I'd spent a decade attempting to master – designing product or service experiences – clients now saw me as a consultant who could advise them on more strategic matters.

As I embarked on this new phase, I became fascinated by how often people leapt straight to solutions without first diagnosing the problem. One company, for example, had a new product that was underperforming, despite them spending heavily on advertising. They assumed the problem was the design of the website landing pages, but had not stopped to ask themselves more fundamental questions. Did people actually want the product? Was it correctly priced? Was the advertising executed well enough to be effective? Did people associate this kind of product with their brand? How did it compare with the competition? Were there adoption barriers that prevented customers from considering it? When I put forward this range of possibilities in an initial meeting, the responses resembled a bizarre shrugging competition.

The more prospects that contacted me, the more I realised that many people had little idea of the root causes behind their problems, or where they should focus their attention to achieve their growth ambitions. They also didn't consider the implications of their decisions beyond their immediate surroundings – their skillset or department was a horizon they couldn't see beyond. Very few, it seemed, considered their business as an interconnected whole.

I had first encountered the value of what they were overlooking – *systems thinking* – in my personal life. I'd been struggling with knee pain for years, and no treatments had worked. Eventually, however, I met a therapist who took a very different approach from the one adopted by the specialists I had previously seen.

She began our first session by explaining how the musculo-skeletal system works as an integrated whole, and how usually 'it is the victims who cry out, not the criminals' when it comes to body pain.[1] Other experts had assumed that the knee was the problem because it hurt. She, however, used her systems approach to trace the problem to its root cause: a muscle imbalance in my hips that put tension on the knee joints. I followed her programme of remedial exercises, the pain disappeared, and to my astonishment I was able to run for the first time in a decade.

These events – both personal and professional – caused a major shift in my worldview. While I still believed that mastering principles *within* a given domain was advantageous, I realised that performance in business was influenced far more by the interactions *between* domains.

Systems thinking offers greater payoffs than discipline-specific principles, because it helps you identify which domain to focus on in the first place. It doesn't make sense, for example, to invest heavily in customer experience improvements if your brand is invisible – people can't have an experience with you if they don't know you exist. Domain-specific skills only offer big payoffs if that domain is a significant performance constraint.

Systems thinking also reduces unnecessary risk by illuminating the broader consequences of decisions. If the knock-on effect of cost-cutting is to lower quality, for example, you end up with inferior products; with inferior products, the brand is likely to suffer, and customers will defect to rivals. Effectively, you have cost-cut your way into less profit – an undesirable outcome. This makes intuitive sense to most people, or may even seem obvious, but common sense and common practice are not the same thing. Improving one aspect of a business at the expense of another happens regularly, and is the underlying cause of many business catastrophes.

The vacuum cleaner manufacturer Hoover, for example, once ran a promotion in the UK offering two return flights to the US with every purchase over £100. As a solution to a particular challenge it proved very successful: a stampede of sales ensued. In systems terms, however, it was a disaster. The offer hadn't been properly costed and turned out to be prohibitively expensive to honour. When Hoover tried to backtrack, the resultant scandal caused huge reputational damage. Their ill-conceived marketing stunt became a financial and PR disaster, and some of Hoover's senior executives lost their jobs as a result.[2]

What I thought was needed was a way to visualise a business as an interconnected whole – a tool or model that could help teams pinpoint performance constraints, collaborate more effectively across specialisms, and minimise the latent risk in their decisions. And as I clung to my childhood belief that there must be an underlying logic to the world, I arrived at an exciting hypothesis: not only is a business a system, every business must be the *same kind of system*.

The underlying factors that determine success must be the same regardless of the business in question, I reasoned, even if their individual configurations are different. So if we could identify a comprehensive but manageable set of these factors and present them on a single page, we could consider how a decision might affect all of them, not just one or two. We could also work through the list to identify the real constraints to performance, and sense-check ideas for new projects or ventures.

My mind caught fire at the prospect, but if I'd known what I was in for I'd have reached for the nearest extinguisher. Five years, 370,000 words of notes and eighty-two iterations later, I finally had a solution that fitted the brief, presented in my second book, *The Grid: The Master Model Behind Business Success*.

The book is in two parts. The first explains the need for a systems thinking approach – introducing the model and how to use it in practice. The second provides a comprehensive primer on each of the elements included within the model – from pricing and regulation, to protecting intellectual property, brand-building and retention strategies – arming the reader with both a comprehensive understanding of how a business works as an interconnected whole, and an appreciation of all the parts that must come together. But while the feedback from readers and experts alike continues to be overwhelmingly positive – many have described it as the most useful book on strategy and decision-making they've read – my euphoria was short-lived.

From consulting engagements and training workshops a

pattern soon emerged. There was something about the apparent obviousness of the factors in the model, combined with how often they were overlooked, that made using the grid an uncomfortable experience for some. On most occasions, when the logic of the grid showed that an idea was unlikely to succeed, the model was abandoned, not the idea. Founders refused to alter their vision. Projects would be finished because they had been started, and insights that could have improved the odds of success were either wholly or selectively suppressed to suit the organisational politics at play.

Our consulting engagements, we came to realise, were less about adding value than adding validation. Companies commissioned our analysis to *defend* hypotheses rather than test them. And data was cherry-picked or manipulated to support rather than inform a narrative. I had always assumed that people wanted their businesses or projects to succeed. What I found instead was subtly different. People wanted to succeed, but *on their own terms* – with their vision, their strategy and their beliefs, and for the most part would rather fail than change them.

These common, if not ubiquitous, behaviours pose a major challenge to management tools and techniques – the grid included – which are predicated on an assumption I'd never thought to question: that we aspire to make rational, objective decisions. But doing so requires a constant battle with our natural inclinations – one we usually lose. In reality, we're more emotional than logical, more intuitive than analytical, often care more about being liked than being right, or are more concerned with politics than productivity. We also prefer to make it up as we go along and learn things the hard way through first-hand experience than to rely on abstract theory or advice.

The psychologist Jonathan Haidt hit the nail on the head

when he said that our conscious reasoning functions like the press secretary, not the president.[3] For the most part we use it to justify and explain the decisions we've already made, not to make better decisions in the first place.

Yet as I ruminated on these challenges, an even bigger realisation dawned on me. Many of the elements within the grid – the factors that determine our business success – are out of our control or can change unpredictably.

We can't know in advance whether people will buy our product, for example. It could easily be too innovative, or not innovative enough. Nor can we know for sure how customers might respond to a price or design change – there could be indifferent acceptance or a backlash. We don't control what our rivals or regulators might do, or whether our customers will stick around – their needs might change, they could emigrate, or die.

When it comes to business, there are so many factors at work that determine our success, so few that are within our direct control, and such dense interconnections between them that we cannot know for certain what the eventual impact of our decisions will be.

While you can design a product, an office, or an organisational structure, *you can't design a successful business*, and the more factors we attempt to manage, the more bureaucratic, dogmatic and slow to respond we become. Similarly, even the most cogent strategy can fail on account of unforeseeable events or difficulties with execution. While frameworks like the grid can help us structure our thinking, form hypotheses, anticipate future scenarios and communicate more effectively, the element of uncertainty can never be expunged. The worldview I'd carried with me from childhood – one where the machinations of the world were fundamentally knowable and first principles paved the way to consistent success – had reached a hard limit.

The irony was profound. In extolling the value of principles and systems thinking, I had unwittingly discovered their limitations. In seeking greater control over outcomes, I had come to recognise the inescapable role of chance. And in providing a means to make more objective, rational decisions, I'd discovered that people tend not to. There was something missing from my worldview.

Some say that when the student is ready, the teacher appears. While grappling with these challenges, I met a quiet Hungarian gentleman – through pure chance, of course – at a party in Los Angeles. We warmed to one another and a close friendship developed.

Over the following years, I learned two things about him. First, he was an extraordinarily successful investor and entrepreneur. Born and raised in Communist Hungary, Csaba (pronounced 'Chabba') launched his first business before turning twenty, importing cars from Italy when the Berlin Wall collapsed. While studying economics at university, he taught himself to trade stocks, bonds and currencies, before going on to run hedge funds around the world, managing money for legendary investors like George Soros. Since then his focus had shifted to tech investments and entrepreneurship. Of his twenty-four early-stage startup investments, several had become unicorns – valued at over $1 billion each.

Second, there was something fundamentally different in our approaches to business. At first I couldn't put my finger on it, but over the course of our conversations it gradually became apparent: our attitudes to uncertainty. Csaba had appreciated three decades earlier than me that the world is inherently unpredictable. But not only had he grasped this essential truth, he had realised that he could turn it to his advantage. The key to his approach – and the missing piece of my worldview – was to think *probabilistically*. To Csaba, business was not an equation to be solved but a numbers game to be played.

He does not, for example, shy away from projects where the odds of success are slim, provided the potential upsides are large enough – a philosophy that many of the world's most successful entrepreneurs live by, but an alien concept to many managers. And accepting that the world is inherently unpredictable, he doesn't attempt to *discover* new business ideas through painstaking upfront analysis as we're taught to do at business school, he *creates them* at minimal cost and commitment through a pragmatic, iterative process.

Appreciating the randomness of the world, he manages his relationships to increase the odds of serendipitous encounters that might create new opportunities – our collaboration on this book being one of them. And in seeking to maximise his payoffs, he balances two distinct approaches to growth: *exploitation* – the structured, incremental kind we're all familiar with; and *exploration* – a form of bounded opportunism that allows him to take advantage of avenues to growth that most of us don't see because we aren't looking.

As I learned more about his methods and mentality, it was as if a missing piece of a puzzle had slotted into place. I found that applying his probabilistic approach didn't invalidate or replace the use of principles or systems thinking; rather it unlocked their full potential by shifting the emphasis towards pragmatic action. It was a strangely liberating revelation.

The quiet tyranny of trying to analyse my way into perfect decisions was replaced by a greater freedom to experiment. I no longer beat myself up if things didn't work exactly as planned and instead began to place my bets accordingly. A fear of failure gave way to a new-found confidence to take action. And as

I more readily followed my instinctive inclination to connect with and help other people, unexpected opportunities began to flow my way.

It struck me that this approach was not only highly effective, it was also more *natural*. We're far more inclined to have ideas and try them out than we are to reverse-engineer solutions from detached, logical analysis. Opportunities tend to arise through our relationships with other people, rather than through cold contrivance. We also learn through trial and error, refining our technique and developing our capabilities as we go. We crawl, walk, run, then run a little faster and further. We don't attend a biomechanics seminar then step onto the starting line of a marathon.

Truth be told, I had no intention of writing another book. I had my hands full with a growing business and had recently become a father. But it soon became apparent just how valuable a book on the topic would be. And as Csaba and I discussed the possibility of collaborating, one thing quickly led to another.

Within just a few weeks of kicking the idea around, we got to work on the project. A new opportunity created as a by-product of a serendipitous meeting, relationship-building and open-minded exploration. The book therefore embodies the lessons we want to share in more ways than one.

It has three parts. Part One develops the central argument: that real-world problems and opportunities cannot reliably be forecast or discovered through analysis because the future is inherently unpredictable and beyond our control (Chapter 1), and that traditional management practices often fail to acknowledge this fundamental feature of reality (Chapter 2).

Some readers may find these two chapters uncomfortable reading. Fortunately, the rest of the book is devoted to practical techniques that can help you make better decisions, create more opportunities and increase your odds of success, as you ground yourself in a better understanding of how the world actually works.

Part Two provides methods and mindsets we can use as individuals. Chapter 3 describes the mindset we must adopt to thrive in an uncertain world. Chapter 4 explores how relationship-building creates a platform for serendipitous encounters – the most common precursor to business opportunities. Chapter 5 then addresses the vital skill of identifying those opportunities and securing commitment to a course of action – in other words, learning to sell.

With these individual skills in place, Part Three extends the ideas to organisations, exploring how to start, grow and manage businesses in our uncertain world (Chapters 6, 7 and 8).

Before I dive in, though, a brief note about how this book was written, and who it was written for.

A common complaint levelled at books by 'do-ers' – entrepreneurs, or CEOs of large companies, for example – is that they are often overly anecdotal. They inspire and entertain, but it can be difficult to apply their insights to the reader's exact situation. By contrast, books by 'thinkers' – academics or thought-leaders in a field – can sometimes seem too rooted in theory and lack practical application, particularly for those whose level of influence in an organisation is limited. A criticism common to both types of author is that their works address either startups and small businesses or large enterprises, but not both.

Fortunately, Csaba and I embody the diversity of experience that you'll find we advocate for in a team. Csaba comes from the world of startups, investment and risk management. He is also a *principal*, with his own money on the line. By contrast, while I've always run my own business, I've spent the majority of my career as an *agent*, advising and designing solutions for corporations, with less personal exposure to risk, but more insight into the machinations of larger enterprises.

Csaba is above all a pragmatist who sees no use in knowledge that can't sharpen his game, and the majority of the ideas in this book come directly from our structured discussions about his ethos and working practice. My own interests are slightly different – I find writing and speaking about ideas as gratifying as applying them – hence my role as the narrator.

In combining our diverse experiences, inclinations and interests, we're thrilled to have created a book that can benefit the full spectrum of business decision-makers, from the leaders and managers of large organisations, to entrepreneurs, would-be founders and more.

If you want to create more opportunities for yourself by improving your mindset, extending your influence, broadening your network and having a better impact on your project work or company's success, you're reading the right book.

Welcome aboard and thank you for joining us.

Part 1
The element of chance

1 Chance encounters
Our unpredictable world exposed

Can we predict the future? The answer isn't as straightforward as you might think.

While we cannot know what will happen on a given day twenty years from now, or what changes may be just around the corner, we inevitably base our decisions on what we think will happen, and outcomes are often reliable. If everything in life were entirely random, we'd never leave the house, and wouldn't feel too comfortable staying at home either.

The problem, though, is that however likely most outcomes seem, they are not certain. As the writer G.K. Chesterton explained, 'The real trouble with this world of ours . . . is that it is nearly reasonable, but not quite. Life is not an illogicality; yet it is a trap for logicians. It looks just a little more mathematical and regular than it is; its exactitude is obvious, but its inexactitude is hidden; its wildness lies in wait.'[1]

Because of these hidden inexactitudes, the world is actually far more unpredictable than we realise. Periods of relative stability are punctuated by apparently random, seismic upheavals. Pandemics, economic meltdowns and new technologies arrive on the scene unbidden. This unpredictability extends to most if not all aspects of life. In 2002, for example, an Australian won

Olympic gold in speed skating when a collision wiped out the leaders on the final corner.[2]

At an intellectual level, most people understand this unpredictability, but in practice they underestimate how prevalent it is. Thus we begin our journey by exposing the hidden wildness of the world, explaining how the fundamental nature of complex systems, human decision-making and technology in particular combine to create an inherently unpredictable environment.

The challenge of complexity

A system is a set of interconnected elements that produces its own patterns of behaviour, and we can think of systems as belonging to one of two basic types: the complicated and the complex.

In a complicated system there may be thousands of interconnected parts, but they obey clear rules which make their behaviour predictable and understandable. A mechanical watch or jet engine, for example, is complicated but operates in a predictable way.

In a complex system, however, owing to the interdependencies between elements or the potential for each element to act of its own volition, the whole doesn't behave as the sum of the parts, which can make its behaviour unpredictable. Why is that?

In 1887, King Oscar II of Sweden offered a prize to anybody who could solve the infamous Three Body Problem, a physics challenge that concerns modelling the movements of three celestial bodies – the Earth, Moon and Sun, for example. The French mathematician Henri Poincaré gave it his best shot and failed – it remains unsolved to this day – but his paper was so impressive that he was still awarded the prize. Poincaré kept noodling away at the problem, and in a revision of his original paper inadvertently laid the foundations for what became known as *Chaos Theory*.

He explained that when elements of a system are interconnected, small errors or changes in calculation are magnified the more they interact – a phenomenon also observed by meteorologist Edward Lorenz over half a century later when running computer simulations to model weather patterns. Lorenz found that minuscule differences – say, measuring variables to four rather than six decimal points – produced radically different forecasts. This observation led him to present a brief paper at a weather conference in 1972, titled, *Predictability: Does the Flap of a Butterfly's Wings in Brazil Set Off a Tornado in Texas?* Hence the popular moniker for this phenomenon: *The Butterfly Effect*.

Central to both Poincaré and Lorenz's theories are two concepts that underpin a great deal of the uncertainty in the world in general and business in particular: first, that our information is always imperfect, and second, that inputs can have non-linear outputs.

The problem of imperfect information

Incomplete or incorrect information poses a challenge to every business decision-maker. Not only does each of us have partial information (especially concerning our rivals' intentions), but the information we do have is mangled by our own interpretation, beliefs and biases, or is distorted en route to us. Bad news in particular is seldom reported accurately, especially as it makes its way up the hierarchy.

And even if we could ensure good information-gathering

and something approaching objective interpretation, we can always rely on our customers to muddy the waters. As the advertising legend David Ogilvy famously remarked, 'The trouble with market research is that people don't think what they feel, they don't say what they think, and they don't do what they say.' A bon mot with serious scientific underpinnings.

The fact is, according to evolutionary biologist Robert Trivers, we have an innate gift for self-deception, much of which is subconscious. We habitually overestimate our intelligence, abilities and attractiveness, actively repress bad memories, and even recall events that never happened.[3] Since we habitually lie to ourselves – ostensibly as a means to better lie to others – it's unsurprising that we cannot put absolute faith in what we're told.

The logical solution would be to rely on objective measurements, but measuring anything beyond the straightforward (the height of a wall, for example) is fraught with challenges and difficulties. Not everything can be measured and the measurements themselves may be inaccurate. You may assign undue importance to certain measurements, misinterpret them, or perhaps measure the wrong things altogether.

The financial historian and economist Peter Bernstein put it best: 'The information you have is not the information you want. The information you want is not the information you need. The information you need is not the information you can obtain. The information you can obtain costs more than you want to pay.'[4] We have no choice, then, but to make decisions on the basis of partial and potentially misleading information, and accept that outcomes will be uncertain.

The challenge of non-linearity

That small events can have disproportionate impacts is a phenomenon our brains instinctively reject, yet one that dominates
the world around us. Traffic flows rapidly, then grinds to a halt
for no obvious reason. Minor fluctuations in the economy exact
significant effects on the availability of credit.[5] The relationship
between satisfaction scores, repurchasing and pricing power is
similarly non-linear.[6]

Examples of apparently trivial events having profound
consequences can be found everywhere, not least in our personal lives. A minor incident in my life illustrates the point
nicely. When I was eighteen, I boarded a train to visit a friend
and began leafing through a newspaper someone had left on
the seat next to me. I'd just finished school and was looking
to earn some money, so when I spotted an advertisement for
what seemed an intriguing job, I decided, on the spur of the
moment, to apply for it. I was offered an interview, secured the
position and, in this way, met my first mentor, who kickstarted
my career.

Had I boarded a later train, sat in a different carriage, or
even taken a different seat in the carriage I did choose; had
I brought a book with me to read, or engaged in some other
distraction, I wouldn't have spotted the advertisement and so
wouldn't have met my mentor. I might well have embarked
on a different career altogether. Had that been the case I
would certainly never have met my business partner, who
would never have introduced me to the mother of my child.
I'd also never have met Csaba, and you wouldn't be reading
this book.

Indeed, when I look back on my life, every significant development has sprung from similarly insignificant events and

encounters. The same, I am confident, is true of every other person on the planet. Trivial occurrences can have profound consequences, and we can never know the ultimate impact of an event until after it has occurred – a key element of another systems phenomenon, known as *self-organised criticality*.

The impact of self-organised criticality

The simplest way to understand this concept is to imagine building a pile of rice, one grain at a time. The pile becomes steeper until the point at which the addition of a single extra grain triggers an avalanche. We can't be sure which grain will trigger the avalanche, though, or how big that avalanche will be, because any of a large number of grains in the pile could be on the verge of toppling at the moment the event actually takes place.

Any additional grain can therefore cause a small, mid-sized or enormous avalanche, or no avalanche at all, *without there being anything unusual about the grain that triggers it*. If we keep adding grains, the pile will continue to grow until the next random collapse. Were we to visualise the height of the rice pile over time, the graph would look jagged and messy. Periods of growth would be interspersed with random avalanches of various sizes.

Such behaviour is not unique to rice piles. It is a pervasive feature of both natural and social systems: earthquakes, forest fires, movie ticket sales, wars, scientific and political revolutions, and economic fluctuations exhibit the same characteristics. There's no telling the magnitude of events in advance, and nothing special about the circumstances that trigger them either way.[7]

Nassim Taleb's seminal book *The Black Swan* (the title is a reference to the colloquial term for an unpredictable, high-impact event) emphasises the pivotal role such events play in our lives. 'A small number of Black Swans explain almost everything in our world,' he writes, 'from the success of ideas and religions . . . to elements of our own personal lives.'[8] History, he explains, doesn't crawl – it jumps, and is shaped by improbable events. We cannot anticipate or assess their significance until after they have happened.[9]

In summary then, the behaviour of complex adaptive systems can be highly unpredictable, not least because social systems – from the economy and society to organisations of all shapes and sizes – are composed of elements with a distinctive feature: a mind of their own.

The human element

Given our unique hopes and dreams, thoughts and feelings, proclivities and preferences, experiences and expertise, there is simply no telling for sure what any individual will do. Add in our interactions and relationships with other people and the picture becomes even more complex.

While we're capable of independent thought and action, we're also influenced by others. Nothing draws a crowd like a crowd, and we naturally want to fit in with our chosen social group – adopting their behaviours, product choices or opinions. Yet we don't merely decide what to do individually, or blindly imitate others. We also attempt to strategise – anticipating what other individuals or organisations might do.

Any given event may therefore develop in a whole host of different ways. Consider, for example, the El Farol Bar Problem, named after a real bar near the Santa Fe Institute, the spiritual home of complexity science. On any given Thursday, people will want to hang out at the bar unless it's too crowded, in which case it will be no fun. As a result, the bar may end up being full because everyone assumes it will be empty, or empty because everyone assumes it will be full.[10] Any event can spark unanticipated outcomes, whether desirable or undesirable.

And, of course, humans make mistakes, too.

The role of human error

Human beings are naturally error-prone. We can be clumsy, forgetful and distracted. We can have the right plan and mess up the execution, or perfectly execute the wrong plan.

When things go wrong in a big way – a plane crashes or a chemical plant explodes – we're quick to point the finger at the individuals concerned, but this is only part of the picture. Instead, errors are often the consequence of situational factors – inadequate training, bad design or shoddy maintenance, for example. And such *latent conditions*, which are present in all systems, are often invisible until they combine with a unique set of contextual factors to trigger an adverse event.[11]

According to Charles Perrow's *Normal Accident Theory*, such incidents are unavoidable. It's not *if* catastrophic events will occur – oil spills (Deepwater Horizon, 2010), nuclear incidents (Fukushima, 2011), explosions at chemical warehouses (Beirut, 2020) or collapsing structures (Surfside, Florida, 2021) – it is *when*. And since they often come about as a result of complex coincidences, they tend to arrive without warning, catching us unawares.

Part of the issue here is that the number of wrong ways to do things tends to vastly outweigh the number of right ones. As error expert James Reason explains, 'The procedures necessary to guide the preparation of, say, minestrone soup can be conveyed in a few sentences. But the procedures necessary to guarantee that this task will be performed with absolute safety could fill several books . . . there is no way in which all the possible combinations of dangers and their related accident scenarios could be anticipated.'

To reinforce the point, Reason offers another example. Consider a bolt with eight nuts that have to be screwed on in a particular sequence. There is only one correct way to assemble them. There are, however, 40,319 ways in which it can be assembled incorrectly.[12] Errors are therefore a pervasive feature of human life, and an inescapable source of uncertainty. And as Perrow's Normal Accident Theory also makes clear, these errors become even more likely when the complexity of modern systems and their constituent technologies are taken into account.

The emergence and impact of technology

Every technology is predicated on a *principle* or underlying idea that produces a particular solution.[13] For the sake of simplicity, let's use the piston engine as an example. The basic principle behind it is that by exploding Jurassic plankton in a certain way, you can move pistons up and down to create rotary motion.

If a technology works and is shown to be commercially or militarily advantageous, rivalry among designers and engineers will push its performance to the limit. Subsystems will then be added to enhance it or to overcome any limitations it may possess – the humble piston engine, for example, acquired such innovations as a turbocharger and fuel injection. Over time these subsystems reach their limits too, mandating their own subsystems, and so the solution becomes increasingly complicated as its performance improves.

Ultimately, the law of diminishing returns sets in, as each

incremental improvement delivers smaller advances that are ever more expensive and difficult to achieve. At that point, the chances are that a wholly new technological principle may arise that will then embark on its own process of elaboration. A jet engine, for example, is not a very complicated piston engine; neither is the motor in a Tesla. These technologies operate on fundamentally different principles.

In theory we can see how technologies are likely to evolve in the short term – they'll get better by getting more complicated until they are replaced with something simpler. We should also be able to spot when new technologies will catch on – we just need to look at which of our existing solutions have reached maturity and what new technologies might replace them. In reality, however, this process is fraught with uncertainty.

By the time a technology reaches maturity, it is locked into broader structures. The planet is dotted with oil rigs and petrol stations, for example, and there are efficient supply chains for manufacturing and maintaining piston engines, making them easy to buy and own. Mature technologies typically outperform nascent ones too, at least in some ways that matter to people.

The attractions of a new technology, therefore, may not be immediately apparent, however promising it may seem. On top of all that there is a certain systemic inertia. We instinctively prefer the familiar to the new, and are encouraged to do so by the vested interests that support what already exists. Consequently, it can be difficult, and sometimes impossible, for new technologies to gain traction. People will continue to prefer to 'stretch' the old, familiar technology to meet their needs until the moment when the new technology is undeniably better, the broader infrastructure problems are solved or regulation favours a new approach. It can take tremendous capital, not to mention risk appetite, to attempt to see this process through.

Further uncertainty stems from the fact that if two new technologies happen to emerge at the same time, it's not necessarily the case that the better one will prevail; the smallest or most random of events – perhaps a favourable article or chance encounter between interested parties – may cause the less promising one to win out. 'The solution that comes to dominate,' writes complexity economist W. Brian Arthur, 'may not necessarily be the best of those competing. It may have prevailed largely by chance.'

When the US Navy looked into ways to cool the nuclear reactors on its submarine and aircraft carriers, it decided that water cooling was the best way to go. There were two reasons for this. First, their engineers had extensive experience of working with pressurised water. Second, they were concerned about the risks of using other cooling materials in an aquatic environment – sodium, for example, explodes in water.

When the US Atomic Energy Commission subsequently found themselves needing a land-based nuclear reactor in a hurry (for political reasons), it was deemed quicker and easier to adapt a reactor design from an aircraft carrier than to design one from scratch. As a result, water-cooled reactors gained an unassailable advantage in the market, even though experts suggest that, both from an economic and technological perspective, they are not the best solution.[14]

Technology adoption, in other words, is highly unpredictable. At any given moment, dozens if not hundreds of viable, nascent ideas will be in circulation, any one of which *might* break through if it happens to occur in the right place at the right time. And while after the event we assume the triumph of a particular technology to have been 'inevitable', one only has to look at our atrocious track record of forecasting technological trends to realise that's rarely how it seemed at the time.

Contemporary experts believed that personal computers, military aviation, television and the Internet would never catch on. Government think-tank The Rand Corporation predicted that by 2020 we'd be chauffeured around by well-trained apes.[15] Even innovators can misjudge the value of their creations. Xerox invented Ethernet, the graphical user interface, and a technology called Interpress that allowed any computer to talk to any printer, yet saw little potential in them.[16] 3Com, Apple and Adobe – who took each of these innovations to market – have done rather well.

Our world is inherently unpredictable

So far, insights from an array of disciplines all point to the same conclusion: our environment is inherently unpredictable. The world of business is particularly susceptible to upheaval, since success is hitched to a tangle of factors that are unpredictable in isolation, let alone in aggregate.

Social trends, emergent behaviours in organisations and the economy, unforeseeable technological innovations, governmental decrees, competitive action and the full spectrum of human behaviour – from the ingenious to the inept, the felicitous to the erroneous – mix and mingle to create the most unpredictable environment of all.

And while it's human nature to believe that there simply must be some hidden mechanism at work we've yet to decode, or some *meaning* behind epic disruptive events, the evidence shows otherwise. There is no predictable pattern to natural disasters. Events that will bend the arc of human history are nigh on impossible to spot before they happen. Bubbles, crashes, booms and busts are features of the economic system, not flaws that can be readily corrected.

Predictability eludes us with every twist and turn, however hard we try.

The vast majority of expert predictions are incorrect, and when they are correct, inconsistently so. And the further ahead we look, the less we can see. When we factor in the dominant role black swans play in life, we may reasonably conclude that what truly matters cannot be predicted at all.

There's a Yiddish proverb that sums it all up: 'We plan. God laughs.' Uncertainty is an inescapable fact of life. And since most events are beyond our control, we arrive at an inescapable conclusion: our actions alone do not dictate the outcomes.

Outcomes = actions + conditions

Our outcomes are determined by both the actions we take and the conditions we take them in. Let's imagine, for example, that you're applying for a job. You might seek expert guidance on polishing your résumé, carefully research the company you're applying to, learn as much as you can about the role, and prepare rigorously by thinking about what kind of questions they might ask you. You might also put in place contingencies for such unpredictable factors as travel delays that would make you late for your interview.

However, many, if not most, of the conditions that determine whether you will get the job remain uncertain. You won't, for example, know the political landscape at the organisation in question, the calibre of the other candidates, or their relationship with the hiring manager. You can never really know your interviewer's personal goals or success criteria for the hire either, or whether you'll have great chemistry with them. They might think you're overqualified or underqualified. These factors are highly uncertain and beyond your control.

Given all this, your actions must therefore include a probabilistic dimension. You might set some cash aside to buy time to find the right role, given that you might need to kiss a few frogs. You could decide to actively build relationships with people who could introduce you to prospective employers. You could opt to apply for two or three positions that would be a good fit.

This example also reveals another vital lesson: when conditions are uncertain – which they always are to some extent – *the smartest decisions can still have unfavourable outcomes*. Chance can cast the deciding vote, either way.

Most of us dread the prospect of failure. Aside from the practical consequences, a torrent of painful emotions – regret, embarrassment, shame, fear of being reprimanded, and even self-loathing – can come to haunt us. Why? Because we assume we are to blame. To most of us, the notion of a good action and good outcome are inseparable from one another, so if we don't succeed, we must be at fault. The idea that a great decision can have a sub-optimal outcome *and still be a great decision* feels wrong.

And yet, in a complex world where unknowable conditions can determine outcomes, failure might just be the hand we're dealt. And in accepting that events are often beyond our control we can reframe our relationship with adverse outcomes and dramatically reduce our suffering as a result (a topic I'll return to in Chapter 3).

Moreover, we can stop fretting endlessly over whether we're following the perfect strategy, theory or prescription for success. Even if there were one, a desirable outcome would not be guaranteed. We must content ourselves with possibilities and place our bets accordingly.

Everything in business is a numbers game

Some people we meet will become close friends, business associates or clients, and others will fall by the wayside. Some of our ideas will be hits and others misses. Some prospects will become paying customers, others won't. Of the newspapers we pick up on the train, some will contain an item that could fundamentally alter the path of our lives, others will not.

Given all these uncertainties and possible pathways, we have two methods at our disposal if we want to improve our chances of success. We can increase the number of people we meet, ideas we test or prospects we pursue – broadening the top of our funnel, if you like. Or we can optimise our conversion rate – increasing the proportion of what goes in at the top of the funnel that has a positive payoff at the bottom.

The focus of most business literature is on the latter. Optimisation gives us a greater feeling of control and creates a more efficient process – both of which are desirable. But given the inherent uncertainties of the world, too much focus on optimisation can be a bad thing.

To demonstrate, let's imagine two companies with fundamentally different attitudes. One has a *deterministic* approach. Its managers believe that with sufficient analytical skill and careful planning they can guarantee success by minimising their exposure to chance. The other company has a *probabilistic* approach. Its managers accept uncertainty as a fact of life and seek to exploit rather than tame chance by playing a numbers game.

Now let's imagine a project is tabled that has a ten per cent chance of success, but that could yield a 100x return on investment if it succeeds. The deterministic managers will almost certainly turn it down. The odds of success are, quite simply, too low. The probabilistic managers, by contrast, might well say a resounding yes, providing they can comfortably afford to explore the idea. In fact, Jeff Bezos – the richest person in the world at the time of writing – used this exact example to illustrate his similarly probabilistic business philosophy.[17]

In a letter to Amazon's shareholders he reinforced the message: 'As a company grows, everything needs to scale, including the size of your failed experiments. If the size of your failures isn't growing, you're not going to be inventing at a size that can actually move the needle . . . We will work hard to make them good bets, but not all good bets will ultimately pay out . . . The good news for shareowners is that a single big winning bet can more than cover the cost of many losers.'[18]

Since in the real world, most of our success comes from serendipity, happy accidents and taking risks with the potential for non-linear payoffs, incorporating a probabilistic approach within our decision-making leads to greater success.

This insight hints at why managers with a formal business education often fail as entrepreneurs, while seemingly inexperienced individuals with street smarts and 'hustle' can be extraordinarily successful. The former are often entranced by deterministic cleverness, but flounder in the face of unforeseen events. They see business as an intellectual contest, and so find the idea of playing a numbers game abhorrent. The latter, by contrast, trade prolonged cogitation for knocking on doors, pressing the flesh and simply trying stuff out. They will often fail but will sometimes get massive payoffs. They win at a numbers game the analysts refuse to play.

The more time I spend with entrepreneurs, investors, and founder-owners like Csaba, the more I see this difference in sharp relief. Traditional managers use calculated cleverness to avoid taking risks. The real winners take calculated risks with supporting cleverness. Rather than try to avoid failure at all costs, the world's foremost investors, entrepreneurs and leaders accept it as a necessary ingredient for greater success. They see uncertainty for what it is – our greatest source of opportunity.

Uncertainty is our greatest source of opportunity

Imagine a world where you, and you alone, could predict the future. Would it be heaven or hell? When it came to making money you might think it was heaven: you could buy the right stocks and back the best startups with no risk whatsoever.

Unfortunately, though, for the world to continue along its predictable track, you too would have to be predictable. You'd be a passenger in life, with no ability to shape events or to build a better future than the one ordained for you.

Now imagine that everyone shared this miraculous ability to discern the future. Things would be even worse. Because everyone possessed the same insights into the future, no individual would enjoy an advantage over any other one. The same would be true if there was a magic formula for business success – once it was widely known, it would offer no comparative advantage.

The brilliant investor Howard Marks takes this line of enquiry to its logical conclusion in one of his popular memos. 'Everyone's forecasts,' he says, 'are, on average, consensus forecasts.' He goes on to explain, 'If your prediction is consensus too, it won't produce above-average performance even if it's right. The problem is that extraordinary performance comes only from correct non-consensus forecasts, but non-consensus forecasts are hard to make, hard to make correctly, and hard to act on.'[19]

Viewed in this way, uncertainty is not the frightening prospect we believe it to be. Instead it gives us the freedom to choose our own path. If the future is unwritten, we can be the ones to write it. Progress, after all, depends on people being willing to take a chance and be rewarded for it, something Communist regimes learned the hard way. Their fixation on centralised planning and control brought social and economic development to a standstill – as Csaba experienced first-hand growing up in Hungary.

We therefore arrive at our chapter's final conclusion: chance is not something undesirable to be eliminated – a wrinkle to be ironed out, or a barrier to be overcome – it is the wellspring of opportunity itself.

With this realisation, the edifice of modern management gives way under an avalanche of unanswered questions. If more factors are beyond our control than within them, why do management theories focus on detailed analysis rather than probabilities? If the factors that truly determine our success often cannot be foreseen – let alone measured – how did we end up with a culture of obsessive quantification?

If change is the only certainty, why is efficiency so readily enthroned, and adaptability so often compromised? And if uncertainty is our greatest source of opportunity, why do we refuse to engage with it? We find answers to these questions and more in Chapter 2.

Chapter summary

- We live in a world of complex systems whose behaviour is inherently unpredictable.
- Since we must act on the basis of imperfect information, outcomes will always contain a degree of uncertainty.
- Black Swan events – combining low predictability with high impact – play a dominant role in shaping our world.

- The evolution and adoption of new technologies are highly unpredictable.
- The broad gamut of human behaviour – from our individual irrationalities and strategies to our herd behaviours – is yet another source of unpredictability.
- Errors and accidents are both unavoidable and largely unpredictable, owing to the complexity of modern systems.
- Events are far more unpredictable than we think. Great actions can lead to adverse outcomes or vice versa, owing to the uncertain, uncontrollable elements in our environment.
- We must therefore seek to exploit rather than tame chance, by acting probabilistically.
- Uncertainty is also our greatest source of opportunity, allowing us to write the future for ourselves.

2 Standing in Taylor's shadow
Our systemic blindness to uncertainty

Once we accept the inherent unpredictability of the world, two burning questions arise. First, if unforeseeable events are ubiquitous, then why do we act as if they aren't? Second, when it comes to business, why do popular working practices assume a more orderly, stable reality than what actually exists?

To unravel these head-scratching mysteries, we must take a trip back through the time tunnel to understand how our species, *Homo sapiens*, and the professional manager – *Homo amministratoris* – evolved, and pinpoint the mismatches between their evolutionary heritage and the realities of the modern world.

We are not, for example, ideally suited to a sedentary habitat with an abundance of calorie-dense foods. Our brains are also optimised for making rapid decisions in simpler yet harsher environments. And while complex, adaptive systems and probabilities may be intellectually understandable, they defy our intuitions. Our brains obscure the world's randomness behind a veil of cognitive illusions.

Your brain on randomness

Modern psychology has shed light on a bewildering array of biases and delusions that distort our judgement, making the very traits that ensured our survival for millennia seem impish or defective in current times. This presents an interesting quandary: how can we hope to thrive in our complex, unpredictable world if our brains are ill-suited to the task?

Fortunately, while these biases are embedded in the structure of our minds, we are also capable of *metacognition* – thinking about what we're thinking – and *cognitive override* – using our intellectual understanding of a situation to correct our course. We are not hopeless cases, and through conscious awareness of these propensities we can exercise better judgement.

Daniel Kahneman's celebrated *Thinking Fast and Slow*, for example, or Rolf Dobelli's *The Art of Thinking Clearly* both explore a broad spectrum of biases and delusions, and suggest how we might compensate for them. It's sufficient for our purposes, however, to limit our coverage to just five psychological factors that blot out most of the world's randomness, starting with perhaps our most powerful impulse of all: the *desire for control*.

Control

A sense of competence and autonomy are among our most powerful motivators – primal needs that reveal themselves almost from birth. At the turn of the twentieth century, for example, psychologist Karl Groos observed how delighted infants become when they discover their actions have consequences: they experience what he termed *pleasure at being the cause* – a simple joy that encourages children to explore the world through play.[1] If infants are for any reason denied this pleasure, they react negatively – something every parent soon discovers.

This instinctive need for control is at odds with our uncertain world, which is dominated by unpredictable events. And because we find uncertainty uncomfortable, we can subconsciously behave as though we're in command, even if we're doing something we know is entirely random, like flipping a coin – a phenomenon referred to as *the illusion of control*.[2]

In fact, many common behaviours exist to banish the unpleasant presence of randomness and unpredictability in our lives. We analyse and strategise. We seek out expert forecasts. And we eagerly adopt products and services that claim to guarantee results – tendencies that marketers, salespeople, con artists and management consultants often exploit.

Yet our desire for control is not the only reason we put so much faith in upfront analysis, strategising and planning. We also believe in these approaches because once events have happened, they immediately seem so obvious. *Surely better analysis would have revealed this challenge or opportunity?* we think. That, however, is just another cognitive trick that obscures the randomness of the world: the *hindsight bias*.

The hindsight bias

We've all experienced this potent delusion in action. If a couple breaks up, we saw it coming all along. When a product or business becomes a great success, it seems obvious what those responsible for it got right. On the flip side, if a decision we make turns out to be wrong, we wonder how we could have been so stupid. The truism that hindsight is 20/20 holds.

Larry Page and Sergey Brin tried to sell Google early on with the intention of staying in school. They approached AltaVista with a proposal for a $1m deal, then Excite for a $1.6m one – neither organisation was interested.[3] Page and Brin clearly believed in their search technology; they would not have pursued it otherwise. But neither they nor the tech companies they talked to saw Google's true potential.

In hindsight, however, Google's miraculous success is easy to account for. Page and Brin's search engine was easier to use than those devised by other companies. The results were more accurate. The interface was less cluttered – it's all so obvious.

The same is true with other spectacular successes. When Tinker Hatfield proposed the design for the Air Max – with a transparent air bubble inspired by the Georges Pompidou Centre in Paris – executives at Nike thought he belonged in a lunatic asylum.[4] Martin Goodman, the owner of Marvel Comics, thought Spider-Man was a terrible idea.[5] Leica spent twenty years working on autofocus technology for cameras, but sold the technology to Minolta after it was deemed unmarketable.[6] Today, the reluctance or scepticism that met these ideas seems laughable. But that's simply the hindsight bias at work.

Why do humans indulge in such wholesale misrepresentations of reality? Some psychologists hypothesise that it's a by-product of adaptive learning – we erase the knowledge we held previously to make room for new knowledge, thereby freeing the memory from having to store two contradictory narratives. Others suggest that we naturally want our understanding of the world to be coherent, so when we are presented with a final answer, we reconnect the dots in new ways to match the outcome.

The dangers of such thought processes are only too apparent, though. Hindsight bias distorts our perception of our own predictive capabilities, deludes us into thinking we know more than we do, wreaks havoc with our risk calibrations, and makes us assume the world is far simpler than it is. By failing to distinguish between what we know now and what we knew then, we mistake a perceived ability to predict the past for an ability to predict the future – a common problem for management theorists. When we know *what* has happened it's far easier to explain *why* it happened, which brings us neatly on to the third compulsion that edits out the randomness of the world: *post-rationalisation.*

Post-rationalisation

Causality is perhaps the most fundamental and easily understood principle in the universe: bang a drum, it makes a sound. Understanding cause and effect is what allows us to make sense of the world. It isn't long, however, before our interest starts to flow the other way. We demand to know *why things happen* – a need that is so powerful that when there are no explanations, we simply make them up.

This compulsion to provide meaningful explanations for events is inescapable. We impose order on the world whether it exists or not, and always have. In ancient times a failed crop might be blamed on an angry god. Today, TV pundits are employed to provide narratives explaining why stocks have gone up or down, even though these movements are often random fluctuations.

Our desire to know the reason for events is unquenchable, and our gift for post-rationalisation keeps on giving. Yet in creating these narratives, we replace random occurrences with logical inevitabilities, and in the rush to provide plausible-sounding explanations we unwittingly expose ourselves to perhaps the most pernicious bias of all when it comes to business: *the halo effect.*

The halo effect

A century ago, while researching how military officers rated their subordinates, psychologist Edward L. Thorndike observed that officers tended to infer a soldier's specific abilities – such as leadership skills, intelligence and fitness – from their general appearance, a phenomenon he dubbed the *halo effect*.[7]

This natural tendency to extrapolate specifics from generalities makes sense if we imagine the environment in which we evolved. By lumping everything together, and guessing about the factors we can't observe from the ones we can, we take a cognitive shortcut and can act more quickly with less mental effort. We also tend to assume that excellence (or its opposite) in one area is replicated elsewhere, which explains why people will heed the opinions of celebrities on topics where they have no expertise.

Neuroscience increasingly supports the idea that our brains work by making constant inferences. Rather than adopting a linear process where sensory information is processed and a behavioural response produced, experts argue that cognition may actually be more of a back and forth, where in response to a stimulus, the brain serves up a 'best guess' which is corrected as additional sensory data is aggregated.[8]

(Incidentally, this is exactly how video is compressed and sent over the Internet. When your YouTube video is buffering, the server is sending a reduced amount of detail to the browser, which then guesses what's missing. The server has identical guessing software on its side and compares the original video to the guess, then just sends the error corrections to the browser – a far more efficient process than sending the whole file.)

Returning to the matter at hand, it's not hard to see how the halo effect can get us into trouble. By inferring unrelated specifics from generalities, or what is immediately visible, we might unfairly assume that a defendant in a trial is guilty because of the way they look. We might also decide to hire – or not hire – someone because of their accent or the way they speak, rather than their actual ability. And when it comes to establishing what has made a business successful or unsuccessful, we often look in the wrong places.

If a company's financial performance is strong, the halo effect leads us to praise everything about that company, from leadership and culture to the customer service it offers and product strategy it has put in place. By the same token, should that company hit a rough patch, the halo effect becomes the *horn effect*. At a stroke, all those characteristics we previously deemed outstanding turn into major weaknesses. Confident, visionary leaders become arrogant and delusional. The entrepreneurial spirit we once lauded was actually reckless risk-taking. In reality, of course, all that has changed is the stock performance.

This natural inclination to fill in the blanks makes it extremely difficult for us to discern what really makes a business successful. Let's imagine we embark on a quest to discover the secrets of superior performance – as many have done before us. It might seem that a logical approach would be to identify some high-performing companies and ask their management what makes them so successful. After all, if anyone knows why particular companies are successful it ought to be the people who run them.

Unfortunately, though, these people will have been as corrupted by the halo effect as everyone else. They might, for example, tell us that employee satisfaction is the key to their greatness. Their people are happy at work, so they do a better job. And, of course, that could be true. But in fact it's quite possible that the opposite is the case: that it's the superior performance that has driven employee satisfaction. As it happens, one study in this area that has been constructed to avoid the halo effect suggests that the latter interpretation tends to be the correct one. People like to work for successful companies, and that success bestows a halo on employees' workplace experiences.[9]

In other words, most explanations of business success are questionable, because they're based on studying businesses that we *already know* are successful, and rely on the insights of individuals who are *aware of their success*. Research participants unwittingly supply a narrative that seems credible in retrospect – one with the randomness airbrushed out, and the halo effect layered on top. It is also influenced by the information they can most easily recall, a tendency known as *the availability heuristic*.[10]

The availability heuristic

When making decisions we tend to rely on the information we can most readily recall rather than the information that may be significant or relevant. Whatever is most recent or looms largest in our minds inevitably takes pole position. If, for instance, we are asked whether a word chosen at random from a prose passage is more likely to begin with the letter R or have R as its third letter, the likelihood is that we will erroneously assume that the former is the case, for the simple reason that it's easier to call to mind words that begin with an R than those where it appears later on in the letter sequence.[11]

This type of cognitive shortcut manifests itself in various ways. We tend to overestimate the frequency of events that are more salient, like political sex scandals or Hollywood divorces, for example. And personal experiences naturally carry more weight than statistical reports or events involving other people.[12]

There are other ways that the availability bias shapes us, too. Since we are far more aware of the skills we have developed and the hard work we've put in to accomplish our successes in life than the more subtle machinations of chance, we naturally emphasise the former and pay less attention to the latter. I dwell on the rewards and challenges of writing, for example, rather than my good fortune to have been born in a country and into a family where education and literacy are valued and available. Linked to this is the fact that since evolution has programmed us to pay most attention to adverse events – difficulties we have faced or barriers we must overcome – we may not notice the good fortune we experience at all.

Economist Robert H. Frank illustrates these traits nicely in his book *Success and Luck* via the analogy of a headwind and tailwind. Ride a bicycle into a strong headwind and it feels far more difficult, yet cycle with a strong tailwind pushing you along and you don't notice it. In fact, you still feel as if you're cycling into the wind. In the same way, we remember the challenges we've overcome on our path to success while remaining blissfully unaware of good fortune's propulsive force.[13]

Given such impulses and biases, it's understandable that we tend to downplay the influence of unpredictable events in business. We simply don't have an innate feel for randomness, probabilities, or the properties of complex systems that shape our modern world. We prefer instead to imagine ourselves as masters of an environment that is within our control.

And yet, while these cognitive biases and delusions explain a great deal of our attitude to uncertainty, they do not explain why many popular management methods also seem to ignore the extensive unpredictability of the world. Instead, we have never been more fixated on data (all of which comes from the past), analysis (which can only be conducted with imperfect information) and developing predictive capabilities (which are woeful at best and likely to stay that way).

The fallacy of scientific management

To understand why this is the case, we must return to the roots of the management discipline – a story that begins with Frederick Winslow Taylor, who brought the concept of analysis to business – and trace its development to modern times.

Taylor's legacy

Taylor was born into a wealthy family in 1856, but rather than becoming a Harvard-educated lawyer as expected, he skipped college and began an apprenticeship at a hydraulics factory. He rose rapidly through the ranks. And as he did so, he noticed a glaring discrepancy between the behaviour of the machines and their operators. The machines were predictable and efficient. Their operators were inconsistent, inefficient and prone to resting, which compromised productivity.

Since Taylor viewed the workforce as fleshy extensions of the factory equipment – there to do, not to think – he enforced rigid working practices and conducted thorough analyses to improve efficiency. That done, he launched an independent consultancy to take his methods to a wider public. He promised prospective clients lower manufacturing costs through process improvements and standardisation, and the practical application of rigorous research.

The most famous of these consulting engagements was with

Bethlehem Steel, where in 1899 he tackled the thorny process of loading pig iron, a case study that became the centrepiece of subsequent sales pitches. According to his account of the challenge that faced him there, the gargantuan steelworks had churned out 80,000 tons of pig iron – about two million bars – which needed a seventy-five-man team to load them onto train carriages to be transported and sold. The system for doing so, however, was riddled with inefficiencies.

Taylor's analysis suggested that a fourfold increase in productivity was possible – loading a whopping 47.5 tons per person per day – if the right process was put in place. He therefore hired a mountain of a man – specifically selected for maximum brawn and minimum imagination – and trained him to become the first pig iron loader to be managed scientifically. Spurred on by the promise of performance-related pay, the man duly achieved Taylor's productivity target and the rest is history.

Or so the story goes.

In reality, there weren't 80,000 tons of pig iron at Bethlehem Steel, there were 10,000. There weren't seventy-five workers, there were nineteen or twenty. And as for the scientifically calculated 47.5 tons-per-day work rate, it was based on the performance of the ten strongest men available working flat out for fourteen minutes, multiplied by waving a wet finger in the air. In other words, Taylor's research wasn't very scientific at all.

When Taylor proposed to the labourers that they should operate at such a ludicrous pace indefinitely for an extra seventy cents per day, they declined in suitably colourful language. Taylor had them all sacked and replaced with another bunch who were too exhausted to continue after the first day. Then it was Taylor's turn to be fired, and all his programmes at Bethlehem were subsequently terminated.

Taylor's experiments may have ended in either failure or fiction, but it did not matter – he'd captured the spirit of the times. America was enthralled with the promise of science and technology and yearned for an approach to business that matched their ideals. Taylor's fervent belief that management was a discipline ruled by exact laws – the philosophy behind his book, *The Principles of Scientific Management* – was an easy sell, especially to the deans of the Ivy League. Universities saw opportunity in the rapidly industrialising world. Taylor's work promised a veneer of academic legitimacy for the business education they now started to offer.

Scientific management was the answer to all their prayers. Business was to be taught as a Newtonian science based on experiments that never worked. And in keeping with the times, corporations would be treated like elaborate clockwork machines. The schism Taylor set up between the bodies on the shop floor and the brains in the executive office was baked into the curriculum. Simultaneously, the academics and consultants placed themselves at the top of the intellectual food chain – promising superior performance to their enlightened clients.

In their fascinating exposé, *Taylor's Pig Iron Tale*, authors Charles Wrege and Amedeo Perroni were quick to point out both the absurd hypocrisy at the heart of scientific management, and its lasting implications. 'That this was wittingly done by a man who could not abide liars and who insisted on the strict observance of even the slightest rule is a sign of aberrant behaviour,' they wrote. 'That this man who behaved aberrantly was also the founder of a system of management which has deeply affected work relationships to this day requires investigation.'[14] You can say that again.

Taylor's basic paradigm remains largely unchanged 120 years later, and many subsequent gurus have paid homage to him as a heroic inspiration. A blind belief in the supremacy of analytics – or *Greater Taylorism*, as the luminary Walter Kiechel called it – has permeated every aspect of the corporation, and employees seldom seize the initiative when unexpected events occur because they aren't allowed.[15] Strategic thinking is still the exclusive purview of the intellectual elite at the apex of the company and their trusted advisors.

This blueprint has stuck, not because it's a perfect match for our complex environment, but because the wrongheaded belief beneath it remains unchanged: that management could become an exact science. But despite the terabytes of data, the sheer intellectual horsepower deployed in its pursuit, and the most ardent desires of the gurus and acolytes since, Taylor's dream of scientific management remains exactly that.

When is a science not a science?

Unlike Ohm's law, for example – a scientific discovery that explains the relationship between current, voltage and resistance in electrical circuits with absolute reliability – for almost every precept in business there are exceptions.

Generally, higher prices result in lower sales. Sometimes, however, they can cause sales to rise. Extending a brand into an unrelated area is foolish, we're told. Yet Aerobie successfully branched out from making a Frisbee-like flying disc for kids to producing a pneumatic coffee machine – the AeroPress – that has sold in the millions.[16] In science, the opposite of a principle that holds is one that doesn't. In business, however, to paraphrase my friend Rory Sutherland, the opposite of a good idea can be an *even better one*.

While there may be certain law-like principles discernible from data, they do not ladder up to a universal prescription for success, any more than understanding the properties of water droplets allows us to control the weather. With so many factors that could determine an outcome, we can never truly know which ones were decisive. And while we can easily run experiments within an organisation, we can't clone a company, change a single variable in one and see what difference it makes. Furthermore, since performance is always relative in business, the act of playing the game changes the rules.

In short, there can be no skeleton key to unlock business success. Experience gained in one competitive arena is often useless in another. And the future probably won't be like the past. Ron Johnson, for example, had tremendous success designing and running Apple's retail stores but his halo shattered at JCPenney, where his brief tenure as CEO was a disaster. And when it comes to entrepreneurship, things are even more hit and miss. A whopping ninety-three per cent of businesses have to change their initial strategy to flourish.[17] As the economist John Kenneth Galbraith remarked, 'There is nothing reliable to be learned about making money. If there were, study would be intense and everyone with a positive IQ would be rich.'[18]

As a result, in business we find ourselves in a strange situation where, while we employ the basic tenets of the *scientific method* – formulating and testing ideas or hypotheses through experimentation – the process itself does not necessarily yield a reliable body of *scientific knowledge* – a general collection of truths that can serve as the basis for predictable action in the future.

This distinction is lost on many, who mistake the apparatus of science – the research, the data and technical-sounding jargon – for the possibility of turning business into an exact science. The two, however, are not the same, as can be demonstrated by applying philosopher Karl Popper's famous acid test, *falsification*, to them.

According to Popper, when it comes to scientific theories, rather than seeking evidence that confirms our claims – as we tend to do in business – we must seek evidence that proves them wrong.[19] Science, he argues, relies not on confirmation but on falsification. If claims are too vague, cannot be tested or are proven false, they are not scientific. Only when they cannot be shown to be false can they be judged to be true.

Outside the scientific sphere, however, such an approach is hard to apply. My horoscope today tells me that I am entering a vibrant period in my life, and it's a great time to begin exploring a new hobby – something I've done, incidentally – but it is not a scientific claim. I can't disprove that I am entering a vibrant period because I can't measure life vibrancy, and I can't test whether now is a great time to explore a new hobby, either. My horoscope does not pass Popper's test. Neither do most business theories. More often than not, the gurus we follow are little more than commercial astrologers.

Consider, for example, Peters and Waterman's business classic, *In Search of Excellence* – a smash hit that has sold over six million copies, turning its principal architect Tom Peters into a celebrity in the process. The basic thesis of the book is that excellent companies have eight particular characteristics. They 'stay close to the customer', for example, and 'stick to the knitting'. Close scrutiny suggests, however, that Peters and Waterman's methodology and insights were as questionable as Taylor's.

Asking people at successful companies what makes them successful, without comparing those companies to a control group of average performers, is all but useless. It's impossible to isolate what might be a halo effect, or what roles are played by hindsight bias and post-rationalisation. Ultimately, therefore, it simply isn't possible to identify what served to distinguish the winners from the losers.[20]

Once what cannot scientifically be proved is removed, what remains are prescriptions for excellence that verge on the platitudinous, and whose untrustworthiness is revealed by the fact that within two years of the book's initial publication, half the excellent companies included in the study were no longer excellent. When investment analyst Michelle Clayman subsequently went 'in search of disaster', she showed that a portfolio of companies that failed to meet Peters and Waterman's exacting criteria actually outperformed the paragons by sixty per cent.[21]

And yet similarly flimsy formulae are eagerly trotted out and embraced in the workplace every year. We're now told, for example, that a business must *have a purpose* to succeed – that the production of a particular brand of socks or ceramic ball-bearings has to be linked to a broader societal mission if they are to become more successful. Yet in reality, many such businesses fail, and many businesses are very successful without one.

To test any grand business mantra, all you have to do is ask yourself three simple questions. First, is doing the opposite viable? If not, you're dealing with a truism that might be a useful reminder of good practice but is unlikely to offer any real-world advantage. Second, is the claim testable? If it isn't, then it's a generalisation that might or might not be correct. Third, can the claim be falsified? If it can be shown not to have applied in a particular circumstance, then it's not an ironclad law. You'll be staggered by how few business theories pass these three criteria.

The question then is how do these spurious trends take hold in the first place if they can so easily be disproven? I've observed a curious cycle in my career that seems remarkably consistent.

The fad cycle

The process begins with the creation of a new idea to sell, typic-ally by a consulting firm, business school academic or research company.

Such ideas need a particular kind of name – ideally combin-ing two abstract, technical-sounding nouns or verbs. 'Design thinking' is a great example, as is 'digital transformation', 'per-formance marketing' or 'omnichannel experience'.

Such ambiguous names are important because they allow their champions to demonstrate twice as much expertise as everyone else, first by defining what the term means (and why other people have it all wrong), and second by earnestly explaining why it's so important.

Once a suitable name has been coined, the next step is to package the concept alongside some credible-sounding data, anecdotes, and ideally a case study or two. We needn't worry too much about the legitimacy of the research, since most people will learn of our concept second-hand, or won't concern them-selves with the details. We need only generate enough buzz to get some more clients onboard.

With the right tailwind, our big idea gains momentum and our mysterious new jargon starts to penetrate the manage-ment lexicon. Now is the ideal time for step three: producing a second round of research to further reinforce the importance of our idea. Ideally it will say something like: *seventy-eight per cent of Fortune 500 leaders see adopting asymmetric servicing* [a concept I just invented] *as a high priority in the next five years*. If possible we'll emphasise how crucial *maturity* is in this field, to frighten people into thinking they're lagging behind.

This leads to step four – the self-fulfilling prophecy. Whether our idea has merit or not, and regardless of whether it fits with a particular context, a mania takes hold whereby sufficient people believing the idea is important makes it so, and our idea becomes the next competitive battleground. As the fad reaches fever pitch, generous budgets appear, and – as if by magic – the consultants are there to cater to the burgeoning demand.

Eventually, however, interest begins to wane. The results are not as good as everybody hoped and, in attracting so much attention, we've also caught the eye of some critical thinkers, who delight in pointing out that the emperor has no clothes. There's no need to worry, though. Soon another idea gains traction and the cycle begins again.

Consider the ascent of management juggernaut Boston Consulting Group. After two years of trying to compete against mighty incumbents like McKinsey, founder Bruce Henderson decided that the firm needed to specialise, but in what exactly? During a Saturday morning brainstorm they settled on strategy – not because the market was crying out for strategic advice, but because it was vague enough for them to define it, making them the de facto experts.[22]

BCG's first idea was the suitably named *Experience Curve*, followed shortly afterwards by the blockbuster concept that propelled them into the spotlight: the *Portfolio Matrix*. This allocates business units to one of four quadrants depending on the growth of their markets and their market share. *Cash cows* have low growth but high market share. *Dogs* have low growth and low market share. *Stars* have high growth and large market share. And *question marks* are in high-growth markets but have low market share. The idea is that once we know which category each business unit belongs to we can manage it more effectively. We can milk the cows, euthanise the dogs, lavish the stars with attention, and do whichever of the three takes our fancy to the question marks.

When this model was first unveiled, the crowd went wild and BCG became a consulting powerhouse. But does the matrix deserve to be taught to hungover students half a century later? Students applying the matrix in one study systematically selected unprofitable investments, and some research suggests businesses that used it generally underperformed compared to those that didn't.[23]

It's not hard to imagine why. One can easily increase market share through strategies that erode profitability – lowering prices for example – and whether a category is attractive or not depends on a great deal more than just its growth, like how easily others can enter that market or how much competition there is. It's perhaps no surprise that Henderson himself described consulting as 'the most improbable business on earth'.[24]

Selling strategy

Can it really be true that strategy itself – the dominant means by which corporations decide what to do and how to do it – was simply dreamed up by consultants as something to sell? Yes and no.

Just as we were able to work in teams for thousands of years before Peter Drucker 'invented' management, the concept of strategy itself predates Boston Consulting Group by several millennia.[25] Sun Tzu's *Art of War*, for instance, arrived on the scene 2,500 years ago. What Henderson and his fellow gurus did was formalise and package the concept into something that could be sold at scale, extending Taylor's basic blueprint into a whole new realm.

First came the *design school*, which emphasised the importance of *fit* between market possibilities and our own capabilities;

an approach first proposed in the late 1950s that still dominates the curriculum and practice of management. In true Taylorist style, command and control is the order of the day – those at the top of the tree must craft the perfect strategy in isolation, then palm it off onto their minions for implementation.

Igor Ansoff's *planning school* – another variation on scientific management – came next, turning the same basic ideas up to eleven, requiring more data, more boxes and more arrows.

In the eighties came Michael Porter's *positioning school*, which put a slight twist on its forebears. Instead of just establishing a fit between the business and the environment, the aim was to pinpoint and occupy desirable positions within the market. As with his predecessors, Porter saw strategy as a creationist rather than Darwinian activity, where analysis reigned supreme. The opportunities are in the market, he believed; we just need to discover them.

As we entered the nineties another approach took hold, not as a wholesale replacement for these prescriptive schools, but as an addendum: improving operations. Gary Hamel, another management guru who thought Taylor walked on water, implored leaders to develop their *core competencies*. They were also encouraged to 'obliterate' activities that didn't add value by the appropriately named Michael Hammer, through *business process reengineering* – the same idea that didn't improve pig iron loading almost a hundred years earlier.[26]

Fast forward to the present day, and little has changed except to heap these ideas on top of one another. In his hit book *Playing to Win*, Roger Martin – hailed as the second-best management thinker in the world – describes strategy as 'A coordinated set of five choices: a winning aspiration, where to play, how to win, core capabilities and management systems.'[27] This appears to be, to all intents and purposes, a rudimentary synthesis of the concepts we've just explored.

If Martin is number two, you might ask, who is number one? That accolade goes to Renée Mauborgne and W. Chan Kim – co-authors of *Blue Ocean Strategy* – whose basic idea is that companies should seek out a competitively advantageous position in a 'blue ocean' of uncontested space – Porter's positioning idea, reflected in a funhouse mirror.[28]

At every step of the way in the evolution of management thinking, the differences have arguably been superficial rather than substantial: at the helm of seemingly every movement has been a guru brandishing another pseudo-scientific playbook; each iteration appears to have maintained Taylor's intellectual apartheid – decoupling thinking from doing, strategy from execution – the assumption being that opportunities are discovered, not made. They must be excavated by the heavy machinery of analysis, a tricky job that requires a cohort of consultants.

The learning school

As one school has given way to another, critics have rightly pointed out what we concluded in Chapter 1. These grand plans – perfectly formulated in the ivory tower – seem all but destined to fail in our complex, unpredictable world. Henry Mintzberg, the best-known of these critics, never tires of pointing out that most of these prescriptions are never even implemented, let alone fruitful. All the pomp and circumstance just slows us down and gets in the way.

By contrast, the central tenet of Mintzberg's *learning school* is incrementalism. Strategy should be more effective and less clever, with a tighter coupling of thinking and doing. Many successful leaders agree. Jack Welch of General Electric, for example, famously advised leaders to 'Forget the arduous, intellectualised number crunching and data grinding that gurus say you have to go through ... forget the scenario planning, year-long studies, and hundred-plus-page reports. They're time-consuming and expensive, and you don't need them. In real life, strategy is actually very straightforward. You pick a general direction and implement like hell.'[29] But if prescriptive strategies are so costly to develop, so seldom implemented and so unlikely to succeed, why haven't they been usurped by a more pragmatic approach? There are three fundamental reasons.

First, consultants and academics are subject to the same biases as everyone else. Our ingenious ability to post-rationalise events allows us to turn emergent strategies into prescriptive ones after the fact.

In one famous example, Boston Consulting Group, whom we met earlier, produced a report for the British government in 1975 explaining Honda's miraculous success selling small motorcycles in the US – a case study that happened to conform perfectly to their intricate models and theories. According to Honda themselves, however, this was mostly nonsense. Their original strategy was to sell big bikes, not small ones, but it ended in disaster. Luckily, the scooters their staff were using to get around Los Angeles attracted a lot of attention, so they sold those instead. It all came down to serendipity and learning, not clever strategy.[30]

Second, the popularity of management concepts depends a great deal on whether they can be monetised or not. Picture the scene as two consultancies are brought in to pitch to a globo-corp looking to grow. Firm A presents their logical process in a slide deck crammed with clever diagrams, charts and return on investment calculations. They promise to banish uncertainty through rigorous analysis, and precisely pinpoint the most lucrative opportunities in the market. First they'll develop a crystalline vision, then they'll execute it flawlessly.

Firm B, on the other hand, offers to help the company try out some ideas and learn as they go. They can't promise a return on investment because it's a jungle out there, suggesting instead that the client works out how much they'd feel comfortable losing if things don't pan out. I think you'll agree Firm B is facing an uphill battle.

The third reason is more insidious, but one that I've observed countless times in large organisations. Any operation of scale is not just a commercial structure, it's a social one too, where status – another innate human desire – matters a great deal. What signifies our social rank within an organisation? There's salary, of course, but that's often kept under wraps. There are job titles too, but they can easily sound more impressive than they are. What really signifies importance is something else: headcount and budget. The more resources we have at our disposal, the higher our status.

By proxy, then, the most important projects are those that cost the most and require the most manpower, not those that can demonstrate the most obvious value. The net result is that it's often easier to get a sprawling transformation or rebranding initiative approved than it is to get a tactical project signed off that could solve a headache overnight. The small but valuable project is too trivial for the power brokers to bother with. By contrast, nothing says 'We're serious about this' quite like getting in the big guns from a famous, and famously expensive, consulting firm.

All things considered, then, it's perhaps no surprise that most expert entrepreneurs ignore this stuff completely. If a successful startup founder describes you as an academic, it's not a compliment. Many mid-sized companies, which are still founder-owned, also don't have the inclination, let alone the budget, to indulge in highfalutin strategy. And when it comes to the largest companies in the world, their sheer size and complexity can make it impossible to tell whether these deterministic approaches, and the consultants that deliver them, add value or not. As one CEO remarked, 'The deliberate strategy is what we present to the shareholders. The emergent strategy is what we actually do.'[31]

Either way, this brief foray into the history of management and business strategy reveals that the approaches we're most encouraged to take by consultants, gurus and academics are those that can be packaged and sold, based on an age-old paradigm that isn't merely obsolete, but was never fit for purpose in the first place. And yet, since its inception, business management has clung to Taylor's mechanistic mindset.

There are clear parallels with the Age of Enlightenment – when intellectuals and philosophers believed the world to be wholly deterministic, with no wiggle room for randomness.

'Throughout the Age of Reason ... chance, superstition, vulgarity, unreason were all of one piece,' writes Ian Hacking, in *The Taming of Chance*. 'The rational man, averting his eyes from such things, could cover chaos with a veil of inexorable laws. The world, it was said, might look haphazard, but only because we do not know the inevitable workings of its inner springs. As for probabilities ... they were merely the defective but necessary tools of people who know too little.'[32]

He could easily have been describing the management profession. Processes, models, frameworks, research techniques, project management philosophies and quests to gather ever more data stem from a similar deterministic delusion – if we just have more powerful tools, if we just have more data, if we just have better processes, we can analyse our way to victory.

But in a complex world, not only is the future inherently unpredictable, if it were predictable we wouldn't actually control it – everything that happened would be preordained. And in clinging to the belief that business must be an exact science, we not only unwittingly disregard the foundation of the scientific method itself – trying stuff out and seeing what happens – we needlessly limit the scope of our activity to what *feels scientific* and prioritise that over more left-field, creative approaches.

We get duped by the packaging rather than the substance of ideas and focus on what can be easily measured rather than what actually matters. We execute the ideas that seem most logical – the same ones that will be obvious to our logically-minded competitors – and use increasingly complicated methods that expose us to greater risks. We're also lulled into a false sense of certainty by precise yet misleading data that leaves us perilously exposed to unforeseeable events.

Worse still, we perceive the serendipity and tinkering behind our greatest successes as aberrations to be post-rationalised, limiting our ability to exploit their potential fully, while ignoring unexpected golden opportunities because they aren't on our meticulous plan.

Yet history teaches us that ingenious inventions and breakthroughs often come about through happy accidents rather than a deliberate discovery process. The phenomenon by which radar detection works, for example, showed up as interference when two US Navy engineers were testing a high-frequency radio. Realising they'd found a way to detect enemy craft, regardless of weather conditions, they petitioned their superiors for funding, who – in-keeping with our predictive capabilities – thought the idea was idiotic.[33] Other examples of happy accidental discoveries include: Play-Doh, cornflakes, Velcro, antibiotics, the Big Bang, Coca-Cola, the microwave oven, X-rays, Teflon, safety glass and Viagra.[34]

In drilling management professionals with dubious theories, inculcating an obsession with analysis, and extolling the virtues of clever plans, we unwittingly encourage them to ignore such serendipitous discoveries, and set them up to fail in our dynamic, messy world. And in desperately seeking to diminish the role of chance through endless analysis and strategising, we end up taking even bigger risks – putting all our eggs in a very fragile basket of pseudo-scientific Power-Point slides.

As Francis Bacon wrote over 400 years ago, however, 'If a man will begin with certainties, he shall end in doubts; but if he will be content to begin with doubts, he shall end in certainties.'[35] To thrive in an unpredictable world, then, requires adopting a different mindset – the subject of our next chapter.

Chapter summary

- We don't have an innate feel for randomness, probability or the properties of complex systems that shape our modern world, preferring to imagine our environment is within our control, and that events have logical explanations.
- *The hindsight bias* – our tendency to see events as having been predictable once they've already happened – distorts our perception of our predictive capabilities, deludes us

into thinking we know more than we do, and wreaks havoc with our risk calibrations.

- Our need to *post-rationalise* events is so powerful that when there are no explanations for outcomes we simply make them up, blinding ourselves to the randomness of the world.

- Once we know that a business is performing well, *the halo effect* causes us to assume the business is brilliant at everything and provides a credible, randomness-free narrative to explain its success.

- Our judgements are often distorted by recent, frequent or especially salient events – a phenomenon known as *the availability heuristic*. Since our hard work and the obstacles we've faced are more readily recalled, this causes us to downplay the role of randomness and pay less attention to our good fortune.

- The history of management also explains a great deal of our attitude to uncertainty – a story that begins with Frederick Winslow Taylor, who brought the concept of analysis to business and believed that management was an exact science.

- There is no skeleton key to unlock success – our experience gained in one competitive arena is often useless in another, and the future probably won't be like the past.

- Most business theories and management concepts are inherently faddish, and their popularity depends more on whether they can be monetised by academics and consultants than on their effectiveness.

- Strategy itself is no exception, and is dominated by prescriptive approaches that are costly to develop, seldom implemented and unlikely to survive contact with our uncertain world.

- By clinging to the belief that business must be an exact science, we often ignore or denigrate the creativity, serendipity and probabilistic thinking behind our biggest successes.

Part 2
Creating your own luck

3 A matter of mindset
Confronting uncertainty head on

Why are some individuals more successful than others? Given our unswerving belief in meritocracy, we tend to think it comes down to talent and hard work. As tennis superstar Rafael Nadal explained in a recent interview: 'I don't think there is any secret [to delivering top performances] other than hard work, dedication and talent.'[1] But what of luck?

Winners in life are typically offended if you suggest they have been lucky – the headwind/tailwind analogy from the previous chapter explains why. Nevertheless, the idea that we can reach the top of the tree without good fortune withers under the slightest scrutiny.

Suppose success was purely a matter of natural attributes, for example. Should we credit ourselves for possessing them? Hardly. We don't choose to be born with feet like flippers that give us a natural advantage in the lap pool, or with enormous hands that can span Rachmaninov's expansive piano chords; nor do we choose how intelligent we are. We describe people with exceptional natural talent as gifted because their abilities are exactly that: a gift. They are granted at birth, not achieved.

Whether such abilities are then discovered and nurtured is also a matter of chance. Could I have become Olympic luge or mogul skiing champion? We'll never know. These are not skills I learned growing up in suburban England. So even if we're lucky enough to possess a talent, manifesting and developing it is largely down to factors such as our family and educational environment, both of which are also beyond our control.

Nadal's tennis talent, for example, was discovered when he was just three years old by his uncle Toni – a professional tennis coach – who then patiently nurtured it: a stroke of good luck if ever there was one, and an advantage not every child with a talent is afforded. 'Without him I'd be nothing,'[2] said Rafael, acknowledging that there might be more to his performance than hard work, dedication and talent alone. In fact, the more competitive an environment – business, professional sports or the arts, for instance – the greater the role of chance becomes.

Take the relationship between talent and financial success, for example. Professor Alessandro Pluchino and his colleagues at the University of Catania created an ingenious computer simulation to accurately reflect the diversity of talent in the real world and track the success of these virtual individuals over a theoretical forty-year period. Their model arrived at the same wealth distribution we see in reality, yet it also showed that those who prospered most in the simulation were not the most talented. 'The maximum success never coincides with the maximum talent, and vice-versa,' concluded the researchers. 'It is evident that the most successful individuals are also the luckiest ones, and the less successful individuals are also the unluckiest ones.'[3]

Does this mean our achievements in life are simply a matter of chance? No. If you lie on your couch all day hoping that something good will happen, you will be disappointed. And there are plenty who have achieved extraordinary success despite great misfortune or lacking the gifts of their peers.

At the opposite end of the spectrum, many start out with the deck stacked heavily in their favour, yet achieve only a fraction of their potential. And however talented we are, we will not improve if we refuse to accept criticism, or wilt when the going gets tough.

Consequently, there is plenty we can do to shift our odds of success, because the beliefs and attitudes that direct our actions are what matter most – *including our beliefs and attitudes about chance events and outcomes.*

Our first practical step is therefore to cultivate the right mindset. One that will help us to discover our natural interests, talents and abilities, develop a work ethic that allows us to fulfil our potential, and – just as essentially – takes into account the inestimable role of chance in life. In essence, we must strive to create our own good fortune – a prominent theme in this chapter and the next – stay cool, calm and collected in times of great uncertainty, and keep our heads when we're dealt a bad hand.

How do we achieve this in practice? By cultivating five attitudinal principles or dispositions that allow us to transcend the uncertainties inherent in our environment: a healthy relationship with failure, a growth mindset, the tenacity to keep trying until we succeed, a commitment to truth-seeking, and the pursuit of mastery.

Principle 1:
Develop a healthy relationship with failure

The basic premise of this book is that the future is inherently unpredictable, and that most events are ultimately beyond our control. We do not live in a world of certainties, but of possibilities and probabilities. And when we accept this reality, we must then confront an important truth: our actions alone do not dictate our outcomes – unanticipated factors beyond our control are at work, and often play a decisive role.

This realisation doesn't pose a problem when results are favourable. If we get the job, win the pitch or launch a successful new venture, we accept the rewards and get on with life, often blissfully unaware that any other outcome was possible. But when results are unfavourable, it's a different matter. Bad outcomes leave a stronger impression on us than good, and the emotional and practical consequences of failure are often unpleasant.[4] To some, the prospect of failure is so painful that it must be avoided at any cost. I know – I was once one of them.

I was raised in a household where excellence was expected and where I was shamed for my frequent shortcomings. I also spent my formative years at a conservative boarding school where a narrow spectrum of activities – none of which I was particularly good at – were highly regarded.

As a consequence, by adulthood I had assimilated a common yet toxic belief that failure wasn't so much something people did as something they were, and that my value as a human being was contingent on my achievements. These pathologies manifested themselves in two ways. First, I subconsciously limited myself to activities where success seemed most likely. Then I pursued those activities with the kind of monomaniacal perfectionism that only the truly terrified are capable of.

Neither tendency is conducive to maximising our potential, as we'll see, and while a moderate fear of failure is a helpful additive, it's a terrible fuel. When you're driven by fear of failure, the more successful you become the more anxious you feel. Like climbing a ladder, the higher you get the more frightening the prospect of falling becomes.

Yet once we appreciate the probabilistic nature of business, we discover the heavy constraints an unhealthy relationship with failure imposes on our potential success. To avoid such shackles, five insights can help us reframe the concept of failure for the better.

1. Our individual sphere of influence is limited

Since most of what occurs in the world is beyond our control, and great decisions do not always end in great results, it makes little sense to punish ourselves when things go awry. Yet much of our fear of failure is driven by a sense of personal responsibility – that we, and we alone, are culpable if events do not work out the way we hoped, a problem exacerbated by the hindsight bias that we all suffer from.

Once we realise that our sphere of influence is limited, and that we can only make decisions with the information we have at the time, we can see unintended outcomes in a new light – as inevitable consequences of operating in a world beyond our control. And when we no longer feel compelled to beat ourselves up every time things don't work out in our favour, the discomfort associated with failure – and the fear it creates – is greatly diminished.

2. The opposite of success is not failure, it's learning

When we try something new, it takes time to develop skills. My son, for example, often stumbled or fell as he learned to walk. I often made mistakes as I learned to play the piano. In neither case would anyone have regarded what we were doing as 'failing'; we were attempting to develop skills that required practice, and a degree of trial and error. The same is true when we formulate a business strategy or launch a new venture. Some of our assumptions are bound to be incorrect or require refinement, and some factors that will affect our success are unknowable in advance. We can only learn what works through iteration and experimentation.

Most of what we perceive as failure is simply the practical consequence of learning and operating in an uncertain environment. If our hypotheses turn out to be wrong, even if we've got all the way to launching a product to find out, we should see these as valuable lessons that can help us improve – a mantra that Thomas Edison lived by. When an assistant moaned that weeks of experimentation had yielded no results, Edison famously replied, 'I have gotten a lot of results! I know several thousand things that won't work.'[5] We must therefore give ourselves and others permission to fail our merry way forward if we're ever to reach our potential, and recognise that a failed project, vision or venture does not make a person a failure themselves.

3. We cannot succeed if we don't try

If we're not prepared to risk failure, we're unlikely to achieve greater successes. The would-be toddler or concert pianist will get nowhere if they aspire to avoid making mistakes at all costs. Remember: we don't need to be great at something to get started, but we do need to get started to become great. We must possess the courage to take the first step and be prepared to learn as we go.

In business – or in life, for that matter – there are two possible sources of regret: things we wish we'd done differently, and things we never did but wish we had. The latter is generally far worse, because its downside is guaranteed. If we try, we might succeed. If we try and fail, we might learn something valuable. If we don't try, we definitely don't succeed or learn anything.

Logically, then, it makes more sense to try something and risk the prospect of failure than never to try at all.

It is no coincidence that two legends from the world of sports – another domain where chance can cast the deciding vote – espouse precisely this philosophy. 'I can accept failure, everyone fails at something,' said basketball star Michael Jordan. 'But I can't accept not trying.'[6]

'You miss one hundred per cent of the shots you don't take,' said ice hockey player Wayne Gretzky.[7] The same is true in business. We cannot allow a fear of failure to become a self-fulfilling prophecy – if we don't try, we fail by default. We have no choice but to take risks, and with those risks comes the possibility of things going awry.

Many of us struggle to fulfil our ambitions – whether it's taking up a new hobby that's always interested us, embarking on a new business venture or changing career – because we can't get off the starting line. We don't know where to begin. The enormity of the work ahead is daunting. We worry about our lack of experience. Our minds fill with reasons to wait for a better time. We keep aiming but never fire. I use the engineering term 'stiction' to describe this problem. A portmanteau of static and friction, stiction is the initial resistance that stops a body at rest from moving – the first barrier we must overcome whenever we embark on something new.

I've found that there are two aspects to overcoming this obstacle that go hand in hand – an intellectual one and a practical one.

The intellectual solution is to recognise that most of the barriers that prevent us from starting are illusory – a mental mirage caused by gazing towards the horizon. As we peer into the future, the way forward is littered with challenges and obstacles we must certainly face at some point, but we feel as though we need to have solved them today to begin. This is emphatically not the case – we do not need to have solved every problem we might possibly face to get started. Indeed, attempting to do so will prevent us from ever taking action. The practical solution that will get us moving is therefore to limit our focus to the one next step that will move us forward.

Maybe you've always dreamed of learning to surf. Google 'surfing lessons' and book a first lesson with an instructor. Maybe you want to change careers. Start by connecting with twenty people on LinkedIn who have the job you want, explain your situation and ask if they can spare a few minutes to answer some questions or offer some advice. Many will ignore you, but some will say yes, and you're now moving forward. As Csaba likes to say, 'The best way to build momentum is by building momentum.' You get started – typically with a single, trivial step – and soon gather pace and confidence.

In 2021, for example, as the Covid-19 pandemic kept me largely housebound, I decided to embark on a bucket-list project: to build a custom motorcycle. With zero prior experience, no tools, and without even a motorcycle licence, some suggested I was overreaching. In reality, by staying focused on the single next step, I never felt overwhelmed by the project. When I made mistakes, I reminded myself that messing up is an inevitable part of learning something new, and gradually built a network of people to coach me when I got stuck. Here's how I began.

First, I found a bike for sale that was a good candidate for my project, bought it and arranged the shipping – all very easy and enjoyable. While I waited for the bike to arrive, I bought and read a couple of books on bike restoration, acquired the basic tools they recommended and the service manual for the bike – also very easy. I took lessons and obtained my licence – something within anyone's grasp with a bit of practice. Then, when the bike arrived, I began disassembling it following the directions in the service manual, taking photos and labelling every part that came off – no skills necessary beyond swinging a wrench, using a screwdriver, snapping some basic photos and putting stuff into labelled bags and boxes.

Before I knew it, the bike was in bits and I was halfway through rebuilding the engine. When stuck, I checked the books (or YouTube), asked a knowledgeable friend or called a professional. There was nothing more to it than that. The only real barriers were time, the money to buy tools and the space to do the work, but even these can be overcome with a little lateral thinking. I know of one person in Munich rebuilding the same bike as mine in a one-bedroom apartment. He keeps parts under the bed and has a very understanding girlfriend.

You can take a similar approach with your particular ambitions – whether it's becoming a black belt in karate, starting a business or anything else. Decide the first logical step, then the next, and keep going, addressing the challenges as they come.

4. Who dares wins

Many are mystified by how seemingly implausible ideas can attract both funding and people willing to work on them. I know I certainly have been in the past. The reason, however, is simple: it's the big, crazy ideas that have the potential for big, crazy payoffs. In other words, there is a strong link between risk and reward.

Consider, for example, the risks Apple took with developing the iPhone, or that SpaceX took with building reusable rockets. Think of Jim Jannard, who started the sports equipment brand

Oakley in his garage with just $300 and built it into a company he sold for $2.1 billion.[8] Rather than retire and take it easy, he then took on another high-risk challenge, launching Red Digital Cinema, a company that made the world's first 4K digital movie cameras.

Yes, the risk of such projects failing may seem to outweigh the advantage of playing things safe. The fact is, though, that if we notch up several failures but achieve one big winner, we will almost certainly end up ahead of the rival who pursued less outlandish visions. If we believe – as we should – that we cannot achieve extraordinary results with ordinary ideas, we must also accept that there will be a risk of failure.

5. If losses are affordable, failure is impossible

However enlightened our attitude, the downsides of failure remain. We can't just bet the farm and risk losing it all, or put our time and money into every idea that comes our way – we'll be bankrupted in no time. We need some kind of guardrail to stop us getting carried away. The solution is the *principle of affordable loss*: we never bet more than we can comfortably afford to lose on a given idea.

Provided we work within the bounds of affordable loss it becomes impossible to fail. Instead, we'll be learning from mistakes that won't ruin us. Indeed, research shows that affordable loss, not return on investment, is what drives the decision-making processes of the world's foremost entrepreneurs, since it opens them to huge potential upsides while limiting their losses.[9]

To calibrate affordable loss, begin by asking a crucial question: *What's my downside?* While it feels natural to concentrate on the potential benefits of a decision, then determine how the odds of success can be maximised, in reality the opposite approach is more effective. It's better to focus on the potential downsides of a decision and how palatable they are, which liberates us to try more things without the pressure of needing to guarantee a result. Inverting my decision-making process in this way has represented the single biggest shift in my mindset since I began my collaboration with Csaba, and I began reaping the benefits almost immediately. Here is one of many examples.

A prospective client in Europe sent my design consultancy business and a handful of competitors a request for a proposal to help them develop a new mobile app. However, it was clear from the brief that their approach to the project was unlikely to succeed. What should we do? The most obvious options were either to submit the best proposal we could, hope to win the work and then persuade them to take a different approach; or simply to decline the engagement. Instead, applying the principle of affordable loss, we came up with a third option.

I called the prospect with an offer of my own. I would fly out to their offices at a time of their convenience, spend a full day explaining our design processes and answering questions from the team, stay overnight at a hotel so we could have dinner and socialise a little, then fly back to California the following day – all at no cost to them.

Let's look at the prospective downsides of this decision. They could just say no on the phone, and we could then decide whether or not to submit a proposal – no downside at all. Alternatively, they could say yes and accept my offer, in which case the worst possible outcome would be to find that we'd spent a few thousand dollars on flights and hotels, lost three productive days on the trip, suffered a little jet lag and not won any work from them. I assessed all these downsides to be affordable losses for the business.

Now let's look at the potential upsides of this idea. First, we would get to meet face to face, see if we had good chemistry and so deepen our relationship. Second, we would get to have a lengthy discussion where we could learn more about their business and how we might help them than we ever could from the brief. Third, they might abandon their competitive pitch, go with our approach and simply give us the project. And fourth, if we explained exactly how to approach the engagement successfully and they still wanted to stick to their plan, we would know we didn't want to work with them anyway.

So what did happen? They eagerly accepted our offer, and we won both that project and some follow-on work, while avoiding a competitive pitch. The return on investment from my little trip was over 3,000 per cent in the first year.

When the prospective downsides and upsides are laid out in this way the decision may seem like a no-brainer – especially since the outcome is now known. The fact is, though, that most other consultancies presented with the same opportunity would never consider such a course of action. In fact, if a prospective client sent a request for a proposal, and your response was to expense a flight halfway round the world to tell them you have a better idea, you'd probably get fired.

Why is that?

Because their goal is to achieve a clear upside at minimal risk, rather than accepting the risk of a given loss in pursuit of a greater but perhaps less likely upside. Offering to travel halfway round the world, according to this logic, is crazy. Simply submitting the proposal they've requested feels like the sensible thing to do. There is no risk of loss beyond the time spent writing and pitching the proposal, even though responding to a proposal request can easily cost more in time and effort than a short trip abroad.

But while it seems logical that we should seek a guaranteed upside rather than focus on the downsides, this approach is inherently limiting, since we needlessly restrict ourselves to activities where the benefits are immediately obvious in the short term and feel readily achievable. We stay stuck in our comfort zone, progressing in small increments, and can never fulfil our potential.

By contrast, if we're content with the possible downsides of a course of action, we are free to experiment more broadly, take on risks that we'd previously have avoided and, in the process, expose ourselves to greater upsides.

Principle 2:
Adopt a growth mindset

According to psychologist Carol Dweck, the central tenet of a growth mindset is the belief that our basic qualities or abilities can change and grow through conscious effort and guidance from others; that our talents and aptitudes are not fixed – they can be improved or altered – and that our true potential is unknowable. The alternative is a *fixed mindset* – a belief that our qualities are immutably set in stone.[10]

The mindset we adopt has an enormous impact on how we live our lives. In areas where we believe our abilities are fixed, for example, we focus on proving rather than *im*proving our capabilities. After all, if we only have a set amount of talent for something, why bother learning or trying to get better? Why take a risk that might show our inadequacies?

A fixed mindset and fear of failure go hand in hand, keeping us within our comfort zone. Where we have a fixed mindset, we avoid or fiercely reject any criticism, since there's nothing we can do about it anyway. Instead, we look for validation for our abilities, or surround ourselves with people who won't show us up.

A fixed mindset, however, is fundamentally incompatible with what it takes to succeed in our uncertain world. If we don't believe that we can learn, improve and overcome challenges, the harsh realities of the market, the ups and downs of the entrepreneurial rollercoaster and the inevitable failures that are part of life will box us in. Every setback, every unfortunate outcome, every wrong hypothesis will feel like a judgement that cuts us to the bone. We'll never fulfil our potential and will struggle to overcome the difficulties that lie before us.

By contrast, with a growth mindset – a belief that we can develop our potential – we focus more on the process that leads to success than on the outcome. We are more receptive to feedback and constructive criticism that can help us improve, and when we fail we are not defined by it – we use the lessons learned to improve our future performance.

This explains why Satya Nadella placed a company-wide adoption of the growth mindset high on the agenda when he took over as the CEO of Microsoft. He attributes much of their subsequent success to this cultural change. 'The learn-it-all does better than the know-it-all,' he said – a claim that's hard to disagree with.[11] But what can we do to cultivate and maintain a growth mindset? First, we must aspire to be coachable. Then we must do our best to keep our ego out of the driving seat.

Be coachable

I can attribute many successful outcomes in life to an ingenious three-step process. Step one: find an expert. Step two: ask them what to do. Step three: do it.

On the surface, this approach sounds so simple, but many

are incapable of following it. Some people ask an idiot what to do, then do it. Or they find an expert and tell *them* what to do. Some even manage to find an expert, ask them what to do, then do the opposite. Yet such behaviours, while common, are counter-productive. We should certainly never hesitate to question dogma, think critically about the advice we are given or triangulate opinions. But learning from trustworthy experts allows us to acquire a grounding in the essential skills and knowledge we need to succeed in many domains, providing us with essential foundations on which to build.

I'm certainly not alone in welcoming the expert advice of others. As we'll see when we explore the entrepreneurial process in Chapter 6, Csaba's first port of call when exploring a new idea is to gather feedback from domain experts who are well placed to critique the vision – allowing him to either reject the concept outright at minimal cost, or to increase the chances of success. You can do the same. When learning a new skill, researching a topic or embarking on a new venture, seek out trustworthy experts who can guide you, rather than learning the hard way.

How can you know if someone is a genuine expert? I use three simple filters. First, do they have a demonstrable track record of expertise that you can validate? Second, can they explain the what and why of their craft in simple, accessible language? And third, are they willing and able to answer questions to your satisfaction? If people have no tangible examples of their successes, hide behind a wall of technical jargon or are unable to answer your questions, it should raise red flags. But when we do find someone worth listening to and learning from, we often face one further challenge that can prevent us from following their advice: the insidious influence of the ego.

Tame your ego

It doesn't always take much. A stranger pushes in front of you at the grocery store. A colleague criticises your work in front of the boss. That friend you asked for feedback hasn't just found a hole in your business idea, they've perforated it.

There's a hot, visceral surge as our ego takes the reins – we're under attack and must defend ourselves. We're not wrong; they just don't get it. Who do they think they are, anyway? Our tone hardens as we begin to justify ourselves or lash out. We've all been there. But the ugly truth is that nothing destroys more value in business than letting our ego call the shots. Instead, we must actively cultivate a rare and powerful skill: the ability to thrive on constructive criticism.

The key is to recognise that *you are not your work*, and to decouple the two in your mind. Did they say they didn't like the business case you wrote, or that they thought you were a loser? Did they reject your manuscript, or did they assassinate your character? Often we respond as if these are one and the same thing, but they're not. There is a huge difference between someone criticising our work and criticising us. Once we recognise that, we'll find withstanding criticism far easier.

So instead of submitting to your first impulse – usually to reject negative feedback, however trivial – you should take a deep breath and ask yourself, *could this help me improve or make the work better?* More often than not the answer is yes. Try to remind yourself that if someone has taken the time to provide considered feedback, they are probably trying to help you improve. Could they have a point? Is it possible that others might think the same? Focus on what will make the work better, and you'll have much more to be proud of in the long run, however much the experience stings in the moment.

If all else fails, remember this: it's better to accept a critique in private from well-meaning friends, colleagues and mentors while you can easily make changes, than to plough ahead and risk getting the same feedback in public when it's too late. With practice, your hide gets thicker, and once you realise how much other people's feedback helps you improve, you'll start to seek out the most savage of critics. Better yet, when people discover how unusually receptive you are to their input, they'll be even more forthcoming with it. Everybody wins.

A challenge remains, however. Accepting feedback and summoning the energy to act upon it is not always easy. The prospect of starting over, changing tack or reworking previous efforts can crush our spirit, yet if we want to fulfil our potential we have no choice – we must persevere.

Principle 3:
Be tenacious

Call it what you will – tenacity, determination, grit – a large part of becoming successful is to keep going until you succeed. This may sound trite. The fact is, though, many give up too readily, or do not understand the connection between uncertainty and perseverance.

It all comes back to the numbers game. If the odds of success are inherently slim because we are pursuing ideas with the potential for outsized payoffs, or we find ourselves in highly competitive arenas where chance events can play a decisive role, then failure, bad luck or at least some unforeseen setbacks are unavoidable. And the bolder our ideas, the more people will be inclined to reject them, at least at first.

When such events occur, we must learn what we can, adjust our activities accordingly and carry on. We cannot allow setbacks, failures, new information, broken beliefs, mistakes, unforeseen events or even temporary plateaus in our development to cause us to give up. These are unavoidable features of the landscape. And success may be just around the next corner. The only way to find out is to keep trudging up the road, taking Churchill's words to heart: 'Never give in, never give in, never, never, never, never – in nothing, great or small, large or petty – never give in except to convictions of honour and good sense.'[12]

It is ever tempting to attribute other people's victories in life to some exceptional talent or privileged circumstance of which we are deprived. There is even a term for it: the *naturalness bias*.[13] But while such explanations may soothe our ego, they do violence to reality, denigrate the achievements of others and, like all manifestations of the fixed mindset, limit our potential. The harsh reality is that life is an endurance sport, and regardless of the domain, those who succeed tend to be those who summon the stamina to keep going.

Examples are legion. J.K. Rowling's Harry Potter books were rejected by twelve publishers.[14] The founders of Sony spent three years searching for a business idea that would work, even considering selling miso soup and building a miniature golf course, before settling on making an electric rice cooker, which didn't take off either. Their first successful product was a voltmeter, funded by repairing radios.[15]

It took James Dyson 5,127 prototypes before his bagless vacuum cleaner worked, and even then every distributor and manufacturer in the UK rejected his idea, leaving him with no choice but to found his own company. Fifteen years passed between embarking on the project and launching the company that bears his name.[16] Today, he is one of the wealthiest individuals in the world.

Tenacity, then, is a crucial determinant of success. But isn't this strength of will something you either have or you don't? Is it actually possible to become more tenacious? The answer according to Angela Duckworth, the world's foremost authority on the topic, is yes – grit can grow.

According to Duckworth's research, paragons of grit have four psychological assets working in their favour: a deep interest or passion for what they're working on; the capacity for structured practice that systematically improves their abilities; a sense of broader meaning that fuels the endeavour; and finally, hope – a belief that the future can be better than the present or past. All of which can be developed over time. 'You can learn to discover, develop, and deepen your interests. You can acquire the habit of discipline. You can cultivate a sense of purpose and meaning. And you can teach yourself to hope,' writes Duckworth.[17]

Developing our grit is a twofold process. First, we must discover those activities which we are intrinsically motivated to pursue by embracing our unique interests and developing a strong sense of self. Second, we must take practical steps to build momentum by setting realistic expectations for what is achievable, and creating routines and rituals that help us screen out distractions and keep moving forward.

Embrace your uniqueness

Human nature is riddled with contradictory, paradoxical behaviours. In the social realm, for instance, we all wish to fit in while also standing out. We cannot succeed in life without cooperating with others, yet we must also compete. We want to be true to ourselves, but are acutely concerned with what other people think of us.

The twentieth-century sociologist David Reisman explored

this topic in his landmark work, *The Lonely Crowd*, drawing a distinction between our innate inner- and other-directedness. More inner-directed individuals, he explained, have a deep appreciation for their own character – an internal gyroscope that provides a stable foundation for action. By contrast, the control equipment for other-directed individuals is more like a radar.[18] They are highly attuned to the actions and interests of others, and blend in with the fashions of the day like a chameleon.

Reisman believed that a rise in consumerism would cause a societal shift towards other-directedness. People would pay greater attention, he wrote, to what famous actors, artists or other entertainers bought and did. I suspect he would be shocked by just how prescient his theory was. Incidentally, Glubb Pasha, who studied the rise and fall of empires, observed that 'The heroes of declining nations are always the same – the athlete, the singer or the actor.'[19] Should we be worried that the only people with over 200 million Instagram followers at the time of writing are literally an athlete, a singer and an actor?[20] A little beyond our scope perhaps, but Reisman had his own concerns about the perils of other-directedness. Those who were overly anxious about the opinions and approval of others would suffer an inability to know what they wanted, while being preoccupied with what they liked.[21] And herein lies the rub.

Uncertainty creates an uncomfortable void that fills easily with other people's ideas – about how we should live or how much we should earn; about who we should be and what success looks like. And as a consequence, we can unwittingly find ourselves living according to other people's success criteria, rather than defining our own.

The problem is, if we're too other-directed – constantly trying to align ourselves with what's in vogue or desperately seeking the approval of others – we are unlikely to discover where our true interests lie. And since tenacity relies on deep, intrinsic motivation, we'll struggle to push ourselves to keep going. Other-directedness has implications for our attitude to failure, too: if our primary concern is looking good to others, we'll be so desperate to avoid failure that we'll never truly flourish. And since other-directedness seeks consensus rather than achievement, it precludes our potential to do or create something extraordinary, to outperform rivals and to fulfil our potential.

Instead of blindly following the pack or fretting about what other people think, we must recognise our unique interests, personality and disposition for what they are: inexhaustible motivators, inimitable assets and vital contributors to the diversity that societies need to thrive. To become more inner-directed is a tremendous advantage then, but doing so requires us to know who we want to be in the first place.

Decide who to be, and what to do comes more easily

Some people believe that the process of individual change, growth or improvement begins with *doing* things differently. If we set the right goals and consciously adopt new behaviours and habits, we'll slowly but surely become the person we want to be. In reality, though, the opposite approach is far more powerful. First, we decide who we want to be, then the behaviours follow. Our sense of identity holds far greater sway over our actions than vice versa, and we naturally behave in a way that is consistent with our beliefs about who we are.

Vegetarians do not eat meat. Non-smokers do not smoke. Jews rest on the Sabbath. To do otherwise would create an uncomfortable cognitive dissonance – a sort of inner turmoil caused by a lack of consistency between what we believe and what we do. Our sense of identity gives us the reason to do things, and when a behaviour is an extension of our persona it becomes automatic.[22]

Our sense of identity also provides a backstop for decision-making in moments of great uncertainty. When there's little data to go on, or we must choose between two sub-optimal directions, we can only illuminate the path forward from within, relying on our values, beliefs and attitudes to guide us. Our sense of identity plays a crucial role in our decision-making then, and if we want to change our behaviour, we must first tell ourselves and others the right story to accompany the transformation. Assume the identity and the behaviour will follow.

James Clear – an expert on habit formation – is explicit on this point. 'True behaviour change is identity change. You might start a habit because of motivation, but the only reason you'll stick with one is that it becomes part of your identity . . . What you do is an indication of the type of person you believe that you are,' he writes. 'When you have repeated a story to yourself for years, it is easy to slide into these mental grooves and accept them as a fact. In time, you begin to resist certain actions because "that's not who I am".' He continues, 'Becoming the best version of yourself requires you to continuously edit your beliefs, and to upgrade and expand your identity.'[23]

Start to call yourself an athlete, entrepreneur or investor and you'll gradually begin to think and act like one. Make a growth mindset a conscious part of your identity, and the inner pressure will force your behaviour in that direction. Remember: your sense of identity is just a set of beliefs about who you are, and beliefs can change. Whatever part of your narrative or identity is holding you back can be replaced with a new story. Above all, you must aspire to live a truthful life – one where your natural inclinations and interests take centre stage – even if your truth is a fiction to others.

The son of two eastern European immigrants, Ralphie Lifshitz was a poor kid from the Bronx who dreamed of the elegant world he saw on the movie screen. We know him today as Ralph Lauren, a new identity described by his biographer as 'a figment of his own imagination' – one that allowed Ralph to shed his baggage and reinvent himself as the living embodiment of the aspirational lifestyle his Polo fashion brand promoted.[24]

Yet however strong our sense of identity and however inner-directed we are, challenges will present themselves that must be overcome. And whether we can surmount them or not depends a great deal on whether we're prepared for such eventualities.

Adjust your expectations

Our expectations determine our perception of any event. I have often dreaded certain things – contacting my Internet provider or making an insurance claim, for example – only to be pleasantly surprised at how painless they were. Yet when it comes to our work, the pendulum can swing the other way – we expect to accomplish far more, in far less time, with far fewer obstacles than is reasonable, and suffer unnecessarily as a consequence.

Take writing, for example. Over the years many people have asked me for advice, or have called seeking solace: their manuscript was rejected by an agent or publisher, they've discovered a chapter doesn't work and needs to be rewritten, or the structure of their book is a mess and they need to start again. It feels as though the sky is falling in. But while these are never fun experiences, once you've been around the track a few times, you know to expect such things – they are inevitable parts of the process for every writer I know.

Unrealistic expectations also cause a great deal of unnecessary pain when starting and growing a business. We expect people to eagerly embrace our innovations, for example – we may even worry about people stealing our ideas. But in reality, most people will shrug apathetically, explain why it will never work, or are happy to settle for existing solutions. As the physicist Howard Aiken remarked, 'If your ideas are any good, you'll have to ram them down people's throats.'[25]

And while people do become billionaires in their mid-twenties, or make lucrative exits a couple of years after starting up, these stories grab the headlines on account of their rarity. The reality is that most serious endeavours take five to ten years to bear much fruit, and during that time there will be soaring highs and crashing lows.

People may ridicule your ideas. Chance events will make a mockery of your plans. You will have to overcome unanticipated obstacles and setbacks. Your assumptions will turn out to be incorrect. But this does not mean you won't succeed. Expecting such adversity – even just expecting the unexpected – makes it easier to take such events in your stride. Prepare for the worst but hope for the best and you'll be well on your way to victory, especially if you can develop a routine that keeps you on the straight and narrow.

Create routines and rituals

Athletes, astronauts and artists have a surprising characteristic in common: they often embrace rigid routines. Many basketball players, for example, are famous for their pre-game rituals, while spaceman Tim Peake emphasises the importance of structure and routine aboard the International Space Station.

Some of the daily rituals that dominate the lives of scientists, writers and composers are famously eccentric. At 11 a.m. each day, Victor Hugo would wash himself on the rooftop of his Guernsey home with icy water left out overnight, scrubbing himself with a horsehair glove. The German poet Friedrich Schiller could not write unless he could smell rotting apples, which he kept in a drawer in his study. Nikola Tesla would mentally compute the cubic volume of each meal before eating it, or he could not enjoy it. Anthony Trollope would write for three hours a day (if he finished a novel during this time, he would immediately start the next). And the celebrated choreographer Twyla Tharp is explicit about the value of repetition, even writing a book on the topic: *The Creative Habit*.[26]

What do the exponents of such different disciplines have in common? First, they face great uncertainty in their environment; second, they must often perform under intense pressure; and third, their work requires periods of deep mental focus.

In such circumstances, repetitive routines or rituals provide a stabilising force that alleviates the stress of the unknown, providing a sense of structure and a feeling of control that is otherwise absent from the environment. Research even suggests that as we become more anxious, our displays of ritualistic behaviour increase naturally to provide a counter-balance.[27]

Daily routines and rituals also help us waste fewer brain-cycles on decisions that don't matter – what to eat for breakfast or when to start work, for example – and allow us to more readily access the mental state where we perform at our best. 'Be regular and orderly in your life,' wrote the novelist Gustave Flaubert, 'so that you may be violent and original in your work.'[28]

Csaba and I are each creatures of habit in our own ways. When writing, for example, I begin as early in the morning as feasible – often at 5:30 a.m. – and write until I've done a thousand words or the clock strikes noon. Csaba's week is broken into a creative block and an action block, he bookends every day with a stretching and exercise routine, and schedules every office hour in advance so he can systematically focus on what matters most.

When structuring your daily routine, I recommend following Cal Newport's advice to distinguish between *deep work* – the immersive efforts that create the most value – and *shallow work* – the kind of humdrum administrative tasks that are less taxing and aren't likely to advance our project, lives or society.[29]

Too many people achieve a fraction of their potential because they allow their time to be sliced so thinly that it turns into vapour. Instead, we must carve out large chunks of uninterrupted time when we perform best for the learning, deliberate practice and experimentation that allow us to systematically master our craft, setting aside time at other points in the day for the tedious administration. We'll get more done, in less time, to a better standard this way.

A vital question remains, however. How do we make sure we aren't persevering with the wrong things? After all, pursuing a flawed idea with heart, body and soul won't make it a success, and when we're pumped up with passion and self-confidence, it's easy to fall in love with our ideas and screen out reality. The antidote is to become insatiable *truth-seekers*.

Principle 4:
Seek the truth

In business as in life, there will always be things we do not know, assumptions that turn out to be untrue, and new information that invalidates our plans. To thrive on uncertainty we must actively assess our information for accuracy, constantly recalibrate our beliefs and seek a plurality of perspectives.[30]

Master investors, entrepreneurs, and others who operate successfully within the realm of uncertainty, therefore tend to share similar virtues: intellectual humility, curiosity about the world and a lifelong commitment to learning. They also incorporate diverse sources of information when making decisions – tendencies we can actively nurture once we're aware of them.[31]

Another vital trait is active open-mindedness. As we explored in Chapter 2, many game-changing innovations or opportunities are discovered by accident or come entirely from leftfield. Albert Hoffman, for example, discovered LSD in 1938 while trying to synthesise a medication to stimulate blood circulation. Testing a sample, he realised something unusual was happening, and promptly rode home on his bicycle – an unforgettable trip.[32]

Steve Jobs – who also took LSD, incidentally – was opposed to the idea that developers would make their own apps for the iPhone, but was persuaded to change his mind.[33] The App Store now supports an estimated $519 billion in trade per year.[34]

As these examples demonstrate, if we cannot keep our minds open to new or alternative ideas, we could miss the biggest opportunities of all. We must therefore seek out those who can provide valuable critiques of our work, challenge our thinking, expose us to a diverse array of new ideas and perspectives, and whose mindset or values inspire us.

Spend time with the right people

Social contagion is an amazing thing. Just by spending time with a certain group of people, or immersing ourselves in a particular culture or environment, we naturally assimilate their norms and behaviours – something I experienced first-hand when I emigrated to Los Angeles from the English countryside almost a decade ago.

It could be that the sunny weather has given me a sunnier disposition. Perhaps the pervasive influence of the creative industries here has rubbed off on me. Maybe because so many people come here to pursue a dream, I've started to dream a little bigger myself. But whatever the cause, I feel a greater sense of optimism and possibility here. People seem less inhibited, more willing to try stuff out, and there's a free-wheeling entrepreneurial spirit that's easy to get swept up in. 'Tip the world over on its side,' said Frank Lloyd Wright, 'and everything loose will land in Los Angeles.' I find that diversity invigorating.[35]

It's not just a matter of place, though, but of people. When I moved here, I didn't know a soul except my partner, but soon made friends through starting a business and joining her social circle, most of whom worked in the entertainment industry. I was naturally influenced by the behaviours, attitudes and energy of these creative, entrepreneurial people, and assimilated subtle yet impactful changes to my outlook that helped me thrive in my new environment.

It is easier to adopt the skills and mentalities you wish to acquire if you spend time with people who embody them, and easier to engage in truth-seeking behaviours when those around you will give you their honest opinions. And if you want to perform better, joining a better team means you'll rise to their level.[36] Before you know it, you'll be on your way to mastery – the ultimate expression of your unique potential and personality, and a pursuit that transcends the uncertainties of the world around us.

Principle 5:
Pursue mastery

I began learning to surf at the same time as my friend Jen, but it soon became clear that we weren't on the same path. I liked surfing – she was consumed by it.

Unlike me, Jen was in the water every day, regardless of the conditions, even if she could only sneak in twenty minutes on a lunch break. If there were no waves, she'd practise paddling. If the waves were bigger than she'd surfed before, she'd find a spot where she could safely push the boundaries of her comfort zone. All she thought about was surfing, and she saved her money for surf camps in other countries where she could experiment with different waves and develop her abilities.

Her consistency paid off and it wasn't long before she was in a different league to me. She paddled faster, caught longer, bigger waves more often, and was far more at ease in the ocean than I was. She also experienced deeper pleasure and fulfilment from her time in the water – it was written all over her face. Jen was on the road to mastery and was reaping the rewards. It was great to watch the process unfold.

The pursuit of mastery – a deep desire to keep improving at something – not only leads us to outperform others, it keeps us pliable and better able to thrive in uncertain conditions, from the currents and swells of the ocean to the movements of the markets. Attaining mastery, however, is not to be confused with perfectionism. In fact, comparing the two sheds light on what makes mastery such an expansive objective, and perfectionism such a debilitating one.

Unlike perfectionism, which focuses on an outcome, mastery is a dynamic process. Perfectionism is driven by fear and anxiety – it keeps us tweaking our product indefinitely but never putting it into the market. Mastery, by contrast, allows us to launch, learn and improve. In fact, the pursuit of mastery weaves together every concept we've explored thus far.

When we're focused on the process, not the outcome, we see failures as learning opportunities. We're free to make mistakes and learn from them, to gather feedback earlier and to experiment. When we're always looking to improve, we're naturally adopting a growth rather than a fixed mindset. It's also far easier to keep going when we see each day's events as small parts of a much grander scheme. And the desire to improve keeps us naturally curious and coachable – mastery and truth-seeking behaviours go hand in hand. It even helps us express our uniqueness and to become more inner-directed.

As Robert Greene explains in his book *Mastery*, the process of mastering a discipline consists of three phases. First comes the *apprenticeship*, where we learn the basics of our craft through a self-directed period of observation, focused practice and experimentation. Then in the *creative-active* phase we begin to apply our own ideas, folding our unique life experience and personality into the mix. Finally, we reach the third and final phase – *mastery* – where we have so deeply internalised the skills and knowledge of our craft that they become reflexive.

We no longer rely on rules and formulas; our intuition has become a finely honed and powerful instrument. We can connect dots that others can't even see, instinctively feel what others must doggedly and deliberately process, and we begin to reshape the discipline in our own image.[37]

As we progress through each stage of mastery, then, we become progressively more inner-directed until our methods and work acquire a recognisable distinctiveness – not through self-conscious contrivance, but through the truthful expression of our unique persona. The pursuit of mastery therefore provides an all-encompassing catalyst to transform our mindset for the better. Yet it also provides recourse for those plagued by a chronic uncertainty of a different type altogether: what to do with our short time on this planet.

I believe that we have been shaped by evolution to find the journey to mastery both deeply pleasurable and meaningful. And that when we discover the thing that truly interests us – awakening to life's task, as Greene calls it – the activity itself becomes the reward.[38] We become more focused, and with that focus the path ahead becomes clear. Fulfilling and stretching our potential, while overcoming countless setbacks in the process, becomes an immensely gratifying process of self-discovery that deepens our confidence and resolve. And as our knowledge grows, so does our appreciation for the craft. The result is a virtuous cycle of continuous improvement. If the meaning of life is to make our lives meaningful, the pursuit of mastery provides us with a unifying purpose.[39]

But why would our evolutionary heritage encourage such behaviour? Aside from the obvious impact on our attractiveness and social standing that comes with exceptional ability, it is because the whole species can benefit from our labour. Society depends on those committed to the pursuit of mastery to solve our most pressing problems, generate opportunities and elevate our culture with their creative works. The pursuit of mastery is not a selfish endeavour, then, it is our gift to the world – an opportunity to contribute to the greater good and a potent source of social capital, topics that take centre stage in the next chapter.

Chapter summary

- To thrive in an uncertain world, we must actively cultivate five attitudinal dispositions: a healthy relationship with failure, a growth mindset, the tenacity to keep trying, a commitment to truth-seeking, and the pursuit of mastery.
- To fulfil our potential we have no choice but to take risks, and with those risks comes the possibility of things going awry. Avoiding failure at all costs limits the scope of our successes.
- We grow by learning, but we learn by doing. To succeed we must take action.
- We can overcome 'stiction' – the barrier to getting started on a new activity – by focusing on the one next step we need to take on the journey.
- When deciding whether to pursue a course of action, the most important question to ask ourselves is: *what's my downside?*
- Adopting a growth mindset – the belief that our basic qualities or abilities can change and grow – is essential.
- We must aspire to be coachable. Learning from experts allows us to acquire the skills and knowledge we need to succeed in less time.
- Recognising the difference between someone criticising us and criticising our work is the key to taming the ego and thriving on feedback from others.
- Perseverance is key. We become more tenacious when working on projects that align with our passions and interests.
- Strive to become more inner-directed. Our unique interests, personality and disposition are inimitable assets.
- To change our behaviour, we first decide who we want to be. The correct behaviours then follow automatically.

- Expecting that things will not always go smoothly makes it easier to take adverse events in our stride.
- Sticking to a daily routine helps keep us on the straight and narrow, while providing a counter-balance to the uncertainties in the world.
- Pursuing flawed ideas with great commitment will not make them a success. We must become insatiable truth-seekers, assessing our information for accuracy, recalibrating our beliefs and seeking a plurality of perspectives, then adjusting our plans accordingly.
- It is easier to assimilate skills and mentalities if we spend time with people who embody them. We rise to the standards of the people around us.
- The pursuit of mastery provides an all-encompassing catalyst to transform our mindset for the better, while providing a sense of purpose that benefits the individual and society.

4 Social capital

The foundation of opportunity in an uncertain world

Every success story has two parts. Story A is a tale of the ups and downs on our way to victory. Then there's Story B: how the people involved came together in the first place, without which there is no Story A.

Once such Story B involves Max Levchin – a bored student squatting at a friend's apartment in Palo Alto – who decided on a hot summer's day to attend a lecture at Stanford by 'a guy named Peter'. Only six people braved the heat to attend, so Max and the speaker got chatting afterwards and decided to meet again for breakfast. That's how Max met Peter Thiel. Together they founded PayPal.[1]

Think of any significant event – how you met your partner, won your biggest client, ended up working with your co-founder or secured your current position – and serendipity will almost certainly have played a role. The implications are simple to grasp: the more interactions you have, and the more people you have them with, the more possibility there is for such opportunities to arise.

That's why Pixar's campus was deliberately designed with a large, central atrium that encourages employees to meet, mingle and have random conversations that might spark new ideas and opportunities to collaborate.[2] Rather than ignoring or denigrating the role of serendipitous encounters, the film-maker facilitates them. We must follow suit if we're to maximise our odds of success.

Even small attempts to connect with more people can have astonishing payoffs because we are seldom more than a few steps removed from anyone else on the planet. As counter-intuitive as it sounds, human relationships fall into a category of mathematical model known as *small-world networks*, where any node can access any other in just a few steps, regardless of how far apart they are. Hence the idea of the *six degrees of separation* – that we are no more than six social connections away from anyone else.[3]

That said, the number of people we meet is irrelevant if we do not behave appropriately during those encounters, or fail to manage our relationships and reputation effectively. 'Trade,' wrote the English philosopher J.S. Mill, 'is a social act.'[4] Our business affairs are governed by the same evolutionary imperatives that make or break relationships in every other sphere of life. Understanding these social instincts, then, is a vital first step.

Our social instincts

For most of our history, our species lived as small bands of hunter-gatherers. The only way to survive was to cooperate with others, most of whom we'd cross paths with regularly.

These two factors – the need to work as a team and the strong possibility of future encounters – are the guiding forces that shaped our social instincts.[5] We not only became a hyper-social species, but one that intuitively manages relationships for the long term. And when we consider these instincts together – our innate inclination to work together and our long-term outlook – many behaviours that seem illogical or even wasteful start to make perfect sense.

Take altruism, for example. Why would we act in a way that benefits others without any obvious payoff for ourselves? According to the evolutionary biologist Robert Trivers, altruism is really a form of cooperation that plays out over the long term.[6] It made sense for early humans to help people they didn't know, because if they were to meet them again in the future and needed help themselves, they might well receive it. This altruistic impulse lives on. If strangers ask us for directions in the street, we stop to help them if we can, even though there's nothing in it for us.

Over time, we evolved emotional rewards and penalties that made such social behaviours instinctive. Interacting with others is our greatest source of pleasure, and it feels good to help our fellow humans – an intrinsic reward that incentivises cooperative behaviour.[7] By the same token, most of us feel unpleasant emotions when we behave antisocially or perceive antisocial behaviour in others. We feel guilt, remorse or shame if we cheat other people, and are outraged when we're treated unfairly.[8] But what is it that makes such righteous qualities so advantageous in the first place? Because they enable trust.

Cooperation in any form, from hunting a bison as a tribe to running a global enterprise, is only possible when there is mutual trust, not only between parties who know and respect each other, but also in such systems as money, and institutions such as corporations or banks. Trust not only makes cooperation possible, it dictates the efficiency of our collaborations – the more we trust one another, the fewer contingencies must be put in place. But challenges still remain. How can we assess whether people are trustworthy before we start working together, for example? From their reputation, of course, but nature has developed another clever solution: *costly signalling*.

Costly signalling

We spend an inordinate amount of time and effort on signalling – to prospective mates, clients or total strangers – about who we are, the social strata we occupy, and our intentions. The problem is that signals can be deceptive, running the gamut from slight exaggerations to outright lies. So to overcome this challenge, many species have evolved to trust signals more when they impose costs on the sender. A stag, for example, demonstrates his strength and fitness by bearing heavy and cumbersome antlers. A peacock sports a large feather train to achieve the same end.

This kind of signalling (also known as the *handicap principle*) underpins a vast array of human behaviour, much of which is automatic.[9] When we smile to have our photo taken, for example, we often tilt our head slightly, thereby exposing our neck. By showing a vulnerable part of the body, we are providing a costly signal that we mean no harm. Similarly, when we are at ease with others, our pupils dilate. This limits our field of view and so makes us potentially more vulnerable – another costly signal.

The same principle is at work in our relationships. How do we test the strength of our bonds with others? We impose costs on them and see how they respond.[10] When we hug someone, for example, we intrude on their personal space and limit their range of movement. We often insult or ridicule our closest friends too – something a stranger would never tolerate. One friend slaps me so hard on the back when we meet I'm amazed he hasn't shattered my spine, and yet I put up with it.

In each case, by imposing and accepting these costs, we signal the strength of our relationship.

Costly signalling also goes beyond direct interactions. In those areas of the world where food is scarce, for example, obesity is a costly signal that demonstrates wealth. In countries where food is abundant, such signalling is ineffective. Instead, being fit and lean is the costly signal, suggesting self-discipline and the means to take care of our wellbeing.

Costly signalling applies in the business world, too. Advertising works in large part *because it is expensive*: if a company is willing to spend so much money to promote a product or a service, it sends a signal to prospective customers that what is on offer must be good.[11] Showing a willingness to expose ourselves to risk works in the same way: the entrepreneur who puts their own money on the line is signalling commitment.

As customers, we like service that is easy and straightforward, but we value it even more if it has been costly or effortful to provide, hence our love of attention to detail and thoughtfulness. And when it comes to communication, the more expensive and effortful it is, the more value we attach to it. We can thank a colleague with a hand-written note or via email. Both will bear the same message. The hand-written note, however, sends a stronger one.

But while these behaviours make intuitive sense – we do most of them on autopilot when left to our own devices – they clash violently with workplace pressures to operate as efficiently as possible and achieve predictable, measurable results in the short term. And by attempting to satisfy these criteria in the social sphere – where inefficiency, serendipity and long-term commitment reign supreme – we adopt behaviours that undermine our ability to build and manage relationships, unwittingly plugging the wellspring of opportunity at its source.

Building social capital

Fortunately, it doesn't take much to tune back into our instincts and adopt a more natural approach to building and managing relationships – one that honours our evolutionary heritage, makes the magic of serendipity work in our favour and leads to greater opportunities. A few practical guidelines will speed you on your way.

Be a host in life, not a guest

When it comes to growing your network, improving the quality of your relationships and increasing the number of opportunities that present themselves, the single most important principle is this: *be a host in life, not a guest.*

Imagine you're a fly on the wall at a fabulous party and observe the perfect host in action. You watch as they carefully navigate the room, making sure everyone feels welcome and has their needs attended to. They pour Beth a Scotch and fix Bill a Martini, just the way he likes it. You also notice that they've deliberately invited people who might benefit from meeting one another, and they make the effort to introduce them. Bob is new in town, so our host introduces him to Brenda, who lives in the same neighbourhood.

You'll notice, too, that the host is generous with their time and attention – they seem genuinely fascinated as Brian describes the different types of loft insulation he's considering buying. And having insisted that nobody should bring anything, they are overwhelmed with gratitude when offered a modest thank-you gift. 'You shouldn't have!' they exclaim, as though they've been given a Fabergé egg, not a box of chocolates.

This vignette reveals the most basic traits of the host mentality: a genuine desire to be helpful with no expectation of reward, attentiveness to individual needs, making others feel welcome and valued, generosity, and connecting people who might be useful to one another. Apply these same precepts to your business relationships – whether with customers, suppliers, colleagues, or anyone else for that matter – and you can't go wrong.

The value of your network will compound over time as you meet and introduce more people. And while the payoffs for helping out will never be clear ahead of time – hosts do not work on a quid pro quo basis – it is human nature to respond in kind to the generosity of others, to reciprocate goodwill and to empower those who create value for us.[12] In fact, the simple act of being a good host can make all the difference to your business success.

Take, for example, the rewards for a minor act of hospitality involving biopharmaceuticals firm Amgen and a biochemist from Chicago called Eugene Goldwasser. Amgen were in deep trouble at the time. Their early product ideas had failed and they were facing intense competition on a project to create a drug to stimulate red blood cell growth. Their one hope lay with Goldwasser, who had worked on the problem for two decades and held the key to success: a tiny vial of protein that contained the code for making the drug, extracted from 2,500 litres of human urine. Eugene, however, was also being wooed by Amgen's main rival, Biogen.

When Biogen's CEO didn't pick up the bill for dinner, Eugene's decision was made. The resulting drug – erythropoietin, or EPO as it's often known – made Amgen $10 billion a year at its peak, a level of success that nobody involved, let alone Goldwasser, predicted.[13]

In a world where we can never know where relationships might lead, it pays to be a good host. Yet we are often guests, too. Others will make introductions on our behalf, or we'll need to introduce ourselves for the first time. And when we do, the way we present ourselves is just as important.

Introduce yourself well

Why do companies try to raise awareness of their products? It's simple: we can't buy things if we don't know they exist or what they do. And the more awareness there is of our product or service, the more prospective customers we reach. The same is true when it comes to creating opportunities through our immediate network. People can only envisage potential collaborations or make beneficial introductions if they know our goals, interests or areas of expertise. And as the number of people who know about our objectives and experience grows, so does the potential for serendipitous outcomes.

The entrepreneur and software developer Jason Roberts captured this idea nicely with his concept of *luck surface area*: 'The amount of serendipity that will occur in your life, your Luck Surface Area, is directly proportional to the degree to which you do something you're passionate about combined with the total number of people to whom this is effectively communicated. The more you do and the more people you tell about it,' he writes, 'the larger your Luck Surface Area will become.'[14]

Notice that Roberts mentions communicating our passions, not our profession – an easy point to overlook, but a crucial one. The more we know about one another, the more likely we are to discover common ground. And the more enthusiastic we are about a subject, the more we'll captivate others with our excitement. In reality, many relationships are formed over a shared personal interest and develop into professional opportunities later.

With this in mind, an easy way to increase your exposure to serendipitous outcomes is not just to put yourself out there a bit more, but to mention your passions, interests or hobbies as well as your job, especially when introducing yourself.[15] A simple example illustrates why this is beneficial. Let's say somebody asks me, 'What do you do?' A standard response might be, 'I run a design consultancy' or 'I'm a venture partner at a VC fund'. But unless people are interested in design or venture capital, there's not much for us to talk about.

If I'm a little more expansive, though, I can increase the potential for discovering common interests quite dramatically. In the course of introducing myself, I might say, 'I run a design agency with my best friend and work as a venture partner for a VC fund in LA. I'm also writing my third book, while trying to make time for my hobbies. I started building a motorbike this year which has been a really fun challenge so far.' Now I've got far more avenues for conversation.

It's unlikely I'll know exactly what will pique the other person's interest. They might be intrigued to know what it's like to run a business with a friend. They might be interested in my previous books or be thinking of writing a book themselves. They might like motorcycles or, if they don't, be curious as to why I would want to build one. They may pick up on my mention of hobbies and find common ground with my whisky collecting, or my love both of classical music and photography, or my interest in running and surfing. By casting a wider net I'm more likely to get interesting conversations going. I'm also more likely to be remembered.

Be memorable

If we want people to remember us when a job or other opportunity is in the offing, or to follow up with us after an initial meeting, we must leave a memorable impression. But we can't do that if they haven't noticed us in the first place. It therefore helps to find ways of being distinctive and memorable both in terms of how we look and how we come across.

Just as brands try to cultivate distinctive assets – colours, shapes, logos or even sounds that are immediately recognisable – we can adjust our own appearance to stand out from the crowd. That doesn't mean we have to dress like Elton John: a striking piece of jewellery, a slightly unusual pair of glasses, even coloured shoelaces can be noticeable and memorable without being off-putting. Steve Jobs' uniform was distinctive but hardly outrageous, for example – round glasses, blue jeans, mock turtleneck, New Balance sneakers. But if we really want to hook people, our personality is our biggest asset.

A number of years ago I attended a lecture by screenwriter David Freeman, who advanced the fascinating theory that the most interesting movie characters, brands and products all possess a dynamic tension he calls *skewed opposites* – combinations of traits that we don't naturally associate with one another – that work to draw us in. Walter White, the chemistry-teacher-turned-drug-kingpin in the hit TV show *Breaking Bad* is a great example. Part of what makes this character so compelling is that we struggle to reconcile the persona of a high school teacher and mild-mannered family man with that of an increasingly brutal drug lord.

Similarly, in their halcyon days, the Danish hi-fi and television brand Bang & Olufsen combined cold, teutonic

aesthetics – glass, metal and sharp angles – with playful interaction design, another compelling skewed opposite. Likewise,
there is something incongruous, to me at least, about Google's
apparent goofiness and the power they wield over our daily
lives, or Warren Buffett's colossal wealth and his avuncular,
modest manner.

I've often reflected on this theory, because everyone I know
has skewed tendencies to some degree. I have a friend who is
often to be seen sitting outside the local cafe with his nose stuck
in some highbrow literature, for example. There's nothing particularly unusual about that, except he reads while sitting on his
race-liveried superbike – a surprising combination. Another
friend is a committed animal-rights activist and vegan who
devotes most of her spare time to supporting the local Buddhist
community. She also smokes cigars and works for a right-wing
think-tank.

Such incongruous, seemingly dissonant traits are a natural part of being human. Yet many of us either don't recognise
them or smother them in an attempt to appear more 'normal'
or conform with stereotypes. This is understandable – it takes
courage to be yourself – but suppressing your uniqueness
almost certainly makes you less interesting to other people. A
little personality can go a long way.

But when we do discover common ground, hit it off with
someone, or an opportunity presents itself, we can't just rely
on other people to get the ball rolling. We need to seize the
initiative.

You go first

Whether it's talking about a difficult topic, suggesting getting together for coffee, launching a new venture, or anything

else that carries an element of uncertainty, people are usually more comfortable responding than initiating. They want to get involved but are waiting for someone else to go first. When I think about how my closest friendships and business relationships have come about, it's often been because I've taken the lead – suggesting we get together then actually following through, rather than either doing nothing, or swapping contact details and hoping the other person will make the first move. In fact, I shudder to think of the amazing relationships I wouldn't now have, had I sat around waiting for things to happen.

We live in a noisy world, full of distractions and competing demands on our time, so it's easy to forget about people and be forgotten in turn. Out of sight is out of mind, so we can't just assume that other people will follow up with us. Instead, we need to seize the initiative ourselves. An initial meeting could go nowhere, but you might end up writing a book together, becoming business partners, close friends, or all three – there's only one way to find out. And taking the lead is just one manifestation of a broader social axiom. When it comes to relationship-building, we get out what we put in.

Pay it forward

If I have observed one consistent trait among not just success-ful people, but *happy* successful people, it is their readiness to help others. Unlike life's guests, who always ask 'What's in it for me?' or want immediate payoffs for their actions, they dem-onstrate a genuine desire to be helpful – whether there's an obvious reward or not.

I think of one friend for example, who always seems to be doing things for other people. I recently attended a party to celebrate forty years of his dental practice and was astonished by the number of well-wishers who showed up. We could barely fit the bottles of wine, golf paraphernalia and other gifts into their living room, and he's a dentist – not exactly everyone's favourite person. I think too about my business partner Ben and his wife Megan, who are much the same. What goes around comes around; it's human nature.

As with other moral and virtuous behaviours that have proved advantageous, reciprocity is instinctive – locked in by emotions such as gratitude for help and resentment towards free-loaders – because it stabilises and strengthens the group.[16] When we're willing to reciprocate, everyone in the tribe benefits from each individual's good fortune and strengths, while offsetting their weaknesses or bad luck.

If our tribe has two hunting parties, for example, and only one is successful each time, it makes sense to share the spoils, rather than for half the tribe to go hungry, or for those who didn't hunt at all to starve to death. And it's this underlying instinct to reciprocate that enables the division of labour, specialisation and mutually beneficial trade that has allowed society to flourish.

Paying it forward doesn't just set the scene for reciprocation. It's yet another example of costly signalling that demonstrates our fitness, depth of resources, expertise or commitment to a given cause – all of which enhance our reputation and make us more attractive partners (in every sense of the word).

In my own business, for example, we often work with free-lancers and independent contractors to help deliver work or provide specialised expertise. Our policy – unlike that of many other agencies or consultancies – is to pay these partners the day the invoice comes in. From a cash-flow perspective this makes less sense than waiting for the standard thirty days to pass, or bullying people into accepting sixty-day terms, but from a social capital perspective the advantages are enormous. We see it reflected in the quality of the work they do, the commitment our partners show to helping our clients that little bit more, their eagerness to talk about our brand to their network, and their willingness to take on work for us when others might be seeking their talents. By contrast, nothing sows the seeds of resentment quite like doing the best job you can, and then being messed around over money. It's not a question of making grand and extravagant gestures, though: small acts and a little extra effort are often all it takes.

Show discretionary effort

A few years ago, while visiting family in Copenhagen, I booked an appointment with a local barber for a quick trim. Since I'm going bald, all I need is a quick buzz to keep things looking tidy, so you'd think that there isn't much scope for a barber to impress me. But my Danish coiffeur did something ingenious that I've yet to experience elsewhere.

Ordinarily, the barber begins by removing my glasses, clips what remains of my hair, then hands back my glasses so that I can admire their handiwork. This time, however, after cutting my hair, the barber produced a small cloth and spray bottle and gave my spectacles a thorough clean. 'I just want everything to be perfect,' he said, as he handed them back to me with a broad smile.

Minor displays of discretionary effort like this are extraordinarily powerful for a number of reasons. First, they enhance our perception of value – improving our opinions of whatever product, service, brand or individual we're dealing with. Second, since we are predisposed to paying attention to unexpected events, they make an experience more memorable and

distinctive. Third, they signal our commitment to the relationship, which deepens trust. And finally, from a commercial
perspective, they can achieve disproportionate results: their
cost is usually trivial so the payoff can be considerable.

Once you get into the habit you'll find opportunities are
abundant. When we submit proposals to clients, for example,
we include the estimated reading time on the cover – a minor
detail that communicates thoughtfulness and often provokes
comment. If I read a book that I think a client or friend might
like, I send it on to them. If I'm grateful for the work someone
has done on a project, I write them a thank-you note. None of
this stuff is clever or extravagant. In fact, my parents would call
most of it 'good manners' – the next topic worth exploring.

Be courteous

Our most painful interactions with companies remind us that,
no matter what activity we're involved in, the basics are the
easiest thing to overlook. I think about my bank, who are no
doubt pouring millions of dollars into machine learning, artificial intelligence and other sexy-sounding stuff, while the daily
essentials – paying someone online or opening a new account –
rank somewhere on the difficulty scale between folding a fitted
bed sheet and landing a helicopter on a moving ship.

The same is true when it comes to relationship-building.
People schmooze at networking events or rack up followers
on social media, but forget the importance of basic courtesies
like saying please and thank you – something I've been taking
advantage of for years as a keynote speaker.

It's no great secret that decent speakers are handsomely
rewarded for their time. Even at the low end – let's say $2,000
for a short turn at the podium – you're still earning many

people's monthly salary in an hour for flapping your jaw up and down about your life's work in a setting where people have no choice but to listen to you. Plainly, this is an immensely privileged position, so you'd expect speakers to be full of gratitude and wonder for the opportunity. They are not.

In fact, the more they get paid, the less grateful they can be, and – irony of ironies – I am typically the only speaker on the roster to send the event manager a thank-you card or gift, even at customer experience conferences. I found this so absurd that I've started performing a little trick to get the message across.

We'll all be waiting in the green room for our turn to present, at which point someone from the event organiser's tech team will come to attach our microphones and escort us to the backstage area. When it's my turn, I'll produce a box of brownies and hand it to them, saying, 'Thanks so much for setting up this amazing event. Can you share these with the rest of the team?' Cue embarrassed shuffling from the gurus in the room as word spreads about the speaker who practises what they preach.

I'd encourage you to find opportunities to do something similar. Like most other examples of discretionary effort, the cost of such courtesies or expressions of gratitude is trivial and the payback often ludicrous – thousands of per cent from a single repeat booking as a speaker, for example, or even more from consulting engagements which can continue indefinitely. Which brings us to another crucial point: we must always treat relationships as a long-term investment.

Treat every relationship as a long-term investment

Many years ago now, I shared a taxi from the airport to an event with another speaker. We got chatting about our presentations and it soon dawned on us that they were spookily similar. When we arrived at the hotel I suggested we meet a little later to compare our sessions in detail. We could make sure they reinforced the same messages, without having too much overlap. It's a good thing we did. They were even more similar than we first thought, and I volunteered to make extensive revisions to my presentation so everyone would benefit.

Four years later, I received a call out of the blue from a prospective client in Ireland, offering us a sizeable design project for a new venture they were launching. The other speaker from the event was on their advisory board and had put us forward for the role. He still remembered me from our brief encounter years earlier. This is not an isolated incident. It's not uncommon for colleagues or former clients to come out of the woodwork after years of radio silence when an opportunity to collaborate presents itself.

Returning to the primary theme of the book, the future is inherently unknowable. We cannot predict where people will end up or when opportunities might present themselves as a result. It could be a decade from now, or even longer. It might be tomorrow. It therefore follows that the only logical approach is to treat relationships as long-term investments. In fact, the worst thing we can do when it comes to managing relationships is evaluate people based on how we might benefit in the short term, and treat them as the next rung on our ladder. People can smell such a strategy a mile off, and aside from the fact that nobody likes to be treated as a meal ticket, it makes you look desperate.

Early in my career I worked at a management consultancy with one memorable individual who was notoriously self-centred. They treated the juniors terribly, hoarded billable hours to line their own pockets at the expense of others, and sought help and cooperation from colleagues only to take all the credit. Years later, however, they applied for a prestigious role at a much larger consultancy, making it all the way to the final interview, only to find one of their former colleagues across the table.

Needless to say, they didn't get the job. Had they taken a long-term view of their relationships – not to mention acted as a host rather than a guest – things might have worked out differently. But even when the shoe is on the other foot – when people wrong us, irritate us or waste our time – we should avoid the temptation to set people straight, lash out or burn bridges. Why? Because relationships aren't our only long-term investment – our reputation is, too.

Guard your reputation

With very few exceptions, growth is slow and decline is fast. A fortune that takes decades to build can be eliminated overnight. We take years to reach maturity as adults, but our demise can be instant. And a reputation that was carefully developed over years can be destroyed with one error of judgement.

Your reputation is like a bank account for social capital. Yet, unlike a bank, where your money is protected with steel and stone, your reputation can shatter like glass and cannot be reconstructed. One ill-timed, impulsive outburst is all it can take to end an otherwise storied career, especially in the social media age, where news travels faster and further than ever before. You must therefore handle your reputation like the aforementioned Fabergé egg – a fragile and precious asset, in other words.

How do you do that in practice? The first rule is simple: if you think you'll need to keep something a great secret to protect your reputation, it is far wiser not to do it in the first place.

Consider, for example, the wasted talents of Jonah Lehrer. A Rhodes Scholar who studied neuroscience at Columbia University, Lehrer wrote a wonderful psychology book – *How We Decide* – along with two other best-sellers. He also contributed to *The New Yorker* and was a successful keynote speaker. Barely into his thirties, he had the world at his feet. When writing his third book, *Imagine: How Creativity Works*, however, he invented several quotes from Bob Dylan, plagiarised another author's work, and lied repeatedly about his transgressions to cover them up.[17]

When his deceptions came to light, his career was over. Two of his books were withdrawn from sale. *The New Yorker* and Wired.com cut ties with him, and his next publication, *A Book About Love*, was savaged by critics who refused to forgive not just his dishonesty but his laziness.[18] It was a tragic waste of a brilliant mind, but an instructive example of how even the smartest and most successful individuals can lose their reputation overnight. To protect yourself against such a calamity, simply ask yourself: Would I want people to know about this? If the answer is 'No,' stop right there.

Another principle to bear in mind – which comes directly from my involvement and writings in the customer experience profession – is to accurately set and then meet expectations.[19] It is breathtakingly obvious that people's expectations determine their perception of the quality of a product, service or interaction, yet we seldom manage these expectations as carefully as we should, and issues can easily arise that tarnish our reputation.

In an organisation of scale, for example, it is easy for expectation issues to cause dissatisfaction. Advertising can make unreasonable claims. Product features or instructions can be confusing or differ from those we had in mind. Gaps between the brand promise and the brand reality can leave customers enraged. Yet generally it is no single person's job to make sure that expectations are set and met accurately along the continuum of customer interactions. Incentives vary by department, and we all suffer the consequences.

The same is true for smaller businesses and individual relationships. As I write, I'm waiting for a sofa to be delivered. The owner of the company told me he'd provide an exact time and hasn't: an expectation set and not met. He is no longer in the cherished *reliable and trustworthy* bucket in my mind – his reputation has been affected.

Expectation issues are so widespread – either because clear expectations haven't been set in the first place, or have been set but not met – that you can stand head and shoulders above rivals just by doing what you say you will, when you say you'll do it, and resetting expectations as early as possible if plans need to change. Nothing is more essential in business than a reputation for reliability and trustworthiness, and often all that is required is a little forethought. Ask yourself: *Am I setting clear expectations? Am I doing what I said I would? Am I keeping people well informed? Do I need to reset an expectation?*

Within my business, for example, often the first thing we ask prospective clients is 'What are you expecting from us?' The answer is normally that they don't know, or if they do, it's seldom what we expect to hear. Asking this question alone can be the difference between embarking on a valuable, satisfactory engagement, or padding down the path to disappointment.

Managing expectations in this way is little more than common sense, but your own life experience probably confirms that it is not common practice. Our last decade helping businesses improve their customer experiences has consistently shown that better expectation management is the quickest, easiest and least expensive way to make everyone happier. That talk is cheap is not always a bad thing.

Be open

It is easy to go through life with our heads down and blinkers on, waiting for our turn to talk instead of listening to what others have to say; restricting our attention to people who have something to offer us here and now. And while we must be strategic and intentional in our relationship-building – our time and energy are precious, as are other people's – simply being open to opportunity can dramatically increase the likelihood of serendipitous events.

It is impossible to write on this topic and not reflect on how the most meaningful and productive relationships in my life have come about. I think of how different things might be if a single call had gone unreturned or question unasked; an introduction not made or interest not shared. Retracing my steps down life's crooked path, I see in sharp relief not only the role of serendipity, but that serendipitous encounters have become opportunities only when I have been open to them and taken action. We never know who will enter our orbit or where a relationship might lead. There's only one way to find out: be open to opportunity.

A decade ago now, I was visiting an old school friend who had returned to the family home after a tour of duty in Afghanistan when I ended up in a heated debate with his younger brother about an obscure psychological theory. I explained that I was planning on writing a book about the foundations behind great customer experiences, and it had come up in my research.

Unbeknownst to me, he was working as an intern for one of London's top literary agents, and he asked if I had a proposal for my book idea. If I did, he'd put it straight on his boss's desk, giving me the one-in-a-thousand chance that it would actually be read. I confessed that I didn't but offered to put one together. He suggested that I hurry up – he was only working there for another week – so that's exactly what I did. I started work on the proposal that evening, and barely stopped to breathe until it was done.

Unsurprisingly, given how hastily it was prepared, the proposal was terrible. The structure was a mess, the ideas were garbled and the prose was clumsy – but it didn't matter. I got it done and met with the agent. He gave me some advice on how to improve it and suggested we keep in touch. This is how my first book came to be. Over the next ten years that agent secured publishing deals for both *The Grid* and the book you're reading now.

It's literally the case – as much as it terrifies me – that if I'd not blurted out my literary ambitions over that cup of tea with my mate's brother, life would look very different. The proposal might never have been written. I might never have secured representation by an agent – certainly not one of his calibre – or have been able to get a publishing deal. The book might have flopped without the advice I received on how to improve it. I probably wouldn't have gained all the life-changing knowledge that's come from reading hundreds of books as background research for my writing efforts.

But while this story illustrates many of the concepts from this chapter in action – the life-changing opportunities that can come from sharing your goals widely, being open to opportunity, seizing the initiative, and cultivating long-term relationships – the role of the proposal and the literary agent in this narrative are not to be overlooked. Opportunities are one thing, outcomes are another. And the magical process of turning one into the other requires another skill we must master to thrive in our uncertain world: selling – the subject of our next chapter.

Chapter summary

- Serendipity plays a crucial role in life's most meaningful events.
- The more interactions you have, and the more people you have them with, the more possibility there is for opportunities to arise.
- Business relationships are governed by the same evolutionary imperatives that make or break relationships in every other sphere of life.
- The guiding forces that shape our social instincts are twofold: our need to work as a group and the strong possibility of future encounters.
- We have developed instinctive emotional reactions that steer us towards moral or virtuous behaviours that enable trust.
- We and other species have evolved to trust signals more when they impose costs on the sender, a phenomenon known as *costly signalling*.
- When it comes to building relationships, deepening trust and improving our communications, the more efficient we try to be, the less effective we are.
- The single most important principle that can help you accumulate more social capital is to be a host in life, not a guest.
- The most basic traits of the host mentality are a genuine desire to be helpful with no expectation of reward,

attentiveness to individual needs, making others feel welcome and valued, generosity, and connecting other people who might be useful to one another.

- An easy way to increase your exposure to serendipitous outcomes is to mention your passions, interests or hobbies as well as your job when introducing yourself. It increases the likelihood of discovering common ground that can lead to interesting conversations.
- Being distinctive and memorable can help you build your social capital.
- We all have incongruous, seemingly dissonant tendencies known as *skewed opposites* that make us interesting. We should embrace them.
- We can't just assume that other people will follow up with us after an interesting initial meeting. We need to take the lead ourselves.
- Pay it forward – 'givers' not 'takers' come out on top in life.
- Minor displays of discretionary effort are extraordinarily powerful. They enhance our perception of value, make us more memorable and distinctive, and deepen trust.
- Basic courtesies or expressions of gratitude are vitally important.
- Treat every relationship as a long-term investment.
- Your reputation is a fragile and precious asset that must be protected. If you wouldn't want people to find out about something, don't do it.
- To build a reputation for reliability and trustworthiness, manage expectations carefully.
- Approach your encounters with others in a spirit of openness – there's no downside!

5 Selling

Bridging the gap from opportunities to outcomes

It has always baffled me why the education system puts such little emphasis on practical skills and knowledge. At school, for example, I learned how oxbow lakes are formed and that King John acquiesced to the Magna Carta in 1215, but not basic money management skills or the constituents of a balanced diet.

Later on, at business school I learned how to do a SWOT analysis and calculate bond yields. But when I set up my own business after graduation I was shocked at how useless my studies had been. I knew nothing about basic administration or tax. Purchase orders and invoices were a complete mystery. Worse still, I'd learned nothing about how to sell.

In the broadest sense, selling is the process of identifying a person's problems or needs, determining and presenting the most valuable solutions to them, and securing commitment to a course of action. It is the means by which we identify and advance opportunities, and is therefore an essential ability to develop in every walk of life.

When you apply for a job you sell yourself to an employer, then negotiate your package. In a creative role you sell your innovations and ideas to your clients and colleagues. And whether you're launching a startup, or the CEO of a successful enterprise, you must sell your vision to investors, team members and customers.

Each of these scenarios – and every other selling situation – has three things in common. First, they are inherently probabilistic. Regardless of your abilities, vision or prowess, selling is always a numbers game. You won't be offered every job role you apply for, or be able to agree mutually beneficial terms. Not every investor will love your vision; it might not fit their portfolio or expertise, and the bolder your ideas the more scepticism you will face. Not every prospect will become a customer – however compelling your offering – for reasons beyond your control: procurement policy, unavoidable switching costs, budgetary constraints, politics, or simply that it isn't the right time – the list is endless. Whatever you're selling – whether it's a skill, an idea or a product – you're effectively filling a funnel from which only a few prospective opportunities at the top will emerge as successful outcomes at the bottom.

Second, there are always unknown or even unknowable factors at work that determine the eventual outcome. For example, we often assume that we understand people's needs when we don't (or not entirely). And there will always be what veteran business consultant Mick Cope calls *surface issues* – topics people share and discuss openly – and *shadow issues* – motivators, thoughts or feelings that people prefer to keep to themselves.[1] As I pointed out in Chapter 1, you'll always have imperfect information that injects uncertainty into proceedings.

Third, however – as with everything else that involves an element of chance – there are ways to increase your odds of success once you acknowledge the inherent uncertainties involved and act appropriately. And the good news is that selling is a skill that anyone can cultivate. You don't need to be a smooth-talking charmer or gifted people-person to get better at it.

To help you on your way, this chapter is organised into five sections. First, I explore the what and why of the sales process from end to end, introducing a model known as *gap selling*. Then I delve a little deeper into four spheres of competence that will serve you well whatever the future holds: *prospecting*, *investigating*, *presenting* and *negotiating*.

Mind the gap

According to sales guru Jim Keenan, the process of selling is all about identifying the gap between where our prospective customer is today – their *current state* – and where they want to be – their *future state* – with the size of this gap determining the value you can create for them. There are three important implications to bear in mind.

First, if you do not understand your customer's current state and their desired future state – whether they're a prospective employer, colleague, investor, or anyone else – you cannot sell to them effectively. This is where most people fall flat on their faces. They focus on themselves or their product, not the customer, talk too much and listen too little. The result? They have no idea what that person actually wants or needs and the probability of a sale drops to zero.

Second, the size of the gap is a matter of perception. A gap that appears small may actually be quite large, or vice versa. To sell effectively, you must help prospects appreciate how big the gap really is, or even find the best gaps to fill. This is where your ability to bring useful insights and ask the right questions becomes paramount, and why the heart of every sale is *building the perception of value that you bring*.

Third, given their desire to move from their current state to an appealing future state, the one constant involved in every sale is change. If people do not want to change, cannot change or do not feel comfortable changing, selling is very difficult. This makes trust, credibility, expertise and relationship management extremely important to the sales process. Not only must you paint a compelling vision of a better future, but your would-be customer must want you as their companion on the journey.[2]

With this in mind, let's return to the generic sales process, which looks like this:

1. **Prospecting.** You begin by identifying prospective customers with problems or needs you can serve, and then contact them. This is a vital first step to building your sales pipeline. If you're not prepared to prospect – to put opportunities in the top of the funnel – you'll struggle down the line.

2. **Investigating.** When you've identified a suitable prospect, the next stage is to remove as much uncertainty as possible by discovering where they are at present and where they wish to be in the future, the size of that gap, and the issues and problems they must overcome to cross it.

3. **Presenting.** Building on the knowledge from your investigation phase, you then conceive and present your solution. This could take the form of a conversation, a written proposal, a pitch presentation, a product demonstration, or all four.

4. **Negotiating.** If your basic sales pitch and the solution you offer are accepted, you now need to negotiate the precise

terms and conditions of the agreement to be reached between the two sides. If all goes according to plan, this phase concludes with a commitment. You land the job, secure the order, strike the deal and pop the cork.

Let's consider these stages in more detail now.

Prospecting

The single most important piece of advice when it comes to prospecting is just to keep doing it. Again, it comes back to the numbers game. The number of deals you can close is a function of the number of prospects you have, multiplied by your ability to convert them. If you convert one in ten prospects to a customer, you must have one hundred decent prospects to make ten sales.

If you don't keep putting more prospects in the top of your funnel, your pipeline will dry up and growth will stall. And since it takes time for a prospect to become a customer, if you don't keep prospecting, you can suddenly find yourself in a position where you've no new customers to serve, and facing a considerable lag between identifying a prospect and the possibility of any revenue coming in.

It's also worth bearing in mind that the hardest time to sell is when you're desperate – prospects can detect your panic from your mannerisms and attitude. You're much better off selling when you're in a comfortable position. This is why continuous prospecting is so important to any business that wants to grow.[3]

So why don't we do it more?

Because it's hard.

The idea of contacting someone we don't know to gauge

their interest in our ideas, products or services is enough to get most people sweating. We don't feel comfortable interrupting people and we don't like being rejected. But it's worth bearing in mind that the worst thing that can happen is simply that someone says no, and they can't say yes if we don't contact them. Remember the mindset lessons from Chapter 3: when it comes to prospecting, your downside is limited but your potential upside is incalculable, and you cannot succeed if you don't try.

I learned these lessons first-hand as a teenager when I took a job selling restaurant vouchers door to door. This sounds like hell to most people, and it certainly had its moments. But in retrospect the experience was invaluable, not least because I learned that the pain of no is temporary. Yes, it can feel unpleasant for a brief moment, but it doesn't cause lasting hurt. We just have to move on to the next opportunity.

When prospecting, the following techniques can prove invaluable.

Prepare thoroughly

It doesn't make sense to contact people out of the blue, willynilly. Instead, you need to be well prepared – a process that begins with developing a target customer profile.

Of course, you can't possibly be sure exactly what challenges or problems any given customer might face. But you do know – or should know – where your products, services or expertise can help. A good starting point, therefore, is to assess exactly what problems you can help with, what the root causes of those problems might be, and what impact they're likely to be having or will have in the future. That done, you can start to identify who might benefit from your knowledge, services or products; which industries, departments or individuals you can help.[4] If you already have a database of happy customers, you can try to discern patterns in it. If you don't, just use your best guess.

Now you have isolated the problems that you can solve and have established who might be experiencing those problems, you need to turn the binoculars around and ask yourself the dreaded question: why should someone buy from you? Most people find this question extremely hard to answer – so much so that many would rather ignore it and suffer the consequences than stop and think about it for a while. Do not succumb to temptation. Instead, put yourself in your buyer's shoes.

In the business-to-business world, if you're targeting a high-value prospect, the chances are that they're besieged with people trying to sell them stuff or get time in their diary; they've already got a roster of preferred vendors, face considerable risks in switching, and must wade through a bureaucratic quagmire to set up a new supplier.

When it comes to consumer goods, there is so much choice that we tend to default to whatever brand we've heard of, is popular with our friends or worked well last time. How can you hope to secure a prospect's interest if there's no reason to choose you? Plainly, you can't, so you must have a compelling reason to be chosen. Better yet, demonstrate the value you can bring by sharing some new ideas.

Offer new ideas

Matt Dixon and his colleagues at CEB (now part of Gartner) made a fascinating discovery when researching top sales performers: it's not relationship-builders, hard-workers or order-takers who perform best, especially with complex sales.

It's *challengers* – people who bring new insights to their customers, make them think and question their assumptions.

These challengers outperform their rivals because they *teach, tailor and take control*, using their superior expertise and understanding of their customer's business or industry to add more value. They aren't afraid to push their customers in a new direction, bring their attention to problems they may not have recognised, and proactively suggest ways to improve their business performance.[5]

You can do the same. Immerse yourself in the industries and markets you serve, conduct your own research, and build your own insights, perspectives and ideas that you can take to clients. Better still, share what you learn along the way on social media to start building familiarity.

Use social media to build familiarity

Prospecting is far easier if people have heard of you or your brand. Familiarity lowers their initial resistance, which gives well-known brands a sales advantage. Whether you love it or hate it, social media has made this easier than ever: share your expertise and start building awareness among prospective customers.

Even if they've never heard of you when you contact them, your prospects are likely to look you up and will find a good-quality network and high-calibre insights reassuring. Better still, your online presence is exactly that: yours. If you change jobs or companies, you don't have to start again – you take your network with you.

I suggest getting into a regular cadence of posting valuable content, replying to comments and engaging with other people's posts on the platform(s) you feel most comfortable with. Light your beacon and see who is drawn to it, maintain a regular presence to stay front-of-mind, and start to build relationships. Over time, the value of your network will compound, your social capital will grow, and it's only a matter of time before opportunities present themselves.

Rehearse and refine

Whatever channel you use to reach out to prospects – knocking on doors, phoning, emailing or social media – it makes sense to know what you're going to say and how they are likely to respond. This means rehearsing and refining your approach as you go – keeping what works and shedding what doesn't until you feel confident entering the fray.

When you do make contact, don't waste time on empty small talk. Get down to business, explaining who you are and why you're getting in touch, ideally in a way that generates some sense of intrigue. It could be that you have a distinctive insight to share, an interesting question to pose, or a way of presenting that appeals to the other side's self-interest.

The aim is simple: the prospect must recognise that you are worth talking to and give you permission to move into the investigation phase. To achieve this, you must be clear on your ask.[6] The odds of success increase dramatically when you are direct, confident and enthusiastic.

Don't say 'no' for your customer

In any selling scenario, we are likely to hear 'no' a lot, which isn't especially fun. So don't make matters worse for yourself by saying 'no' on a prospect's behalf – a lesson I wish I'd learned earlier in life. If somebody doesn't reply, doesn't answer the phone or suddenly goes quiet, we often take it as outright rejection. In reality, however, it takes far more interactions or 'touches' to generate a sale than many of us realise – often ten or so.[7]

So while we don't want to hound people and irritate them, we definitely don't want to say no for them either. I've found that it can sometimes take up to two years of regular check-ins and chit-chats to secure a client. Given the uncertainties in the environment, you never know when needs might change, a buying window might open or the timing might be right – you need to take a long-term view.

Ask for referrals

Finally, an easy way to improve your prospecting is to ask for referrals. If you have an existing roster of satisfied clients, there's no harm in asking them to make introductions to other people they know with similar needs. The chances are that they'll be happy to do so.

Investigating

The aim of prospecting is to get somebody to the point where we can discover how we might help them – the crucial investigation stage. Unless we have a comprehensive understanding of their problems and aspirations, we cannot propose a compelling solution and will face a barrage of objections and obstacles. It's no wonder then that research shows the investigation stage is the most important part of the selling process and the predominant focus of high-performing salespeople.[8]

Fortunately, there are only two skills involved: asking the right questions and listening to the answers. Let's start with the listening.

Active listening

When other people talk, we often don't listen. We may *hear* what they say, but we're actually a million miles away, either because our own inner monologue is drowning them out, or we're thinking of what we want to say next. Just think about how often we interrupt other people and they interrupt us, or all the times we finish people's sentences rather than letting them talk. Few of us are as good at listening as we like to think – I know I could certainly improve. Yet the ability to truly listen is extremely valuable because, as counter-intuitive as it sounds, the way we listen *affects the quality of other people's thinking*. Why is that?

As my friend Nancy Kline explains in her book, *Time to Think*, when we listen patiently, we give people the time to access and develop their own thoughts and ideas. By contrast, when we interrupt people, instead of having the headspace to let their thoughts gestate, provide detailed answers and allow their ideas to take shape, they rush them out half-baked. By becoming better listeners, we increase the odds of our customers sharing valuable insights and ideas.[9]

Three simple tips can make you a better listener: maintain eye contact to show your attention, refrain from interrupting and avoid rushing to fill the quiet. If the other person falls silent for a moment, chances are they are thinking. Giving them the space to gather their thoughts can only be to our benefit, especially if they're answering our questions, the topic we'll turn to now.

Ask the right questions

A few years ago I took a road trip north from New York into the Berkshires, a beautiful area in rural Massachusetts. I stopped along the way at a charming little town called Lenox, where I found myself wandering into the local bookshop.

As I entered the store, the owner came out from behind the counter and struck up a conversation. He asked what had brought me to town and whether I was looking for anything in particular. As our dialogue began to flow, he asked more questions about my reading habits – what kinds of books I liked, what I'd read recently and whether I had any favourite authors.

As I answered, he scampered around the shop, plucking books that he thought I'd like from the shelves, and before I knew it I was at the till with five books that I was genuinely excited to read. One of those books was *Footnotes from the World's Greatest Bookstores*. That little bookshop in Lenox – in business since 1964 – is the first one featured in the book. Given my experience as a customer, I'm not surprised.

This story illustrates a fundamental point that sales experts agree on: there is a strong connection between asking questions and successful selling. The more questions you ask, and the better those questions are, the more likely you are to complete a sale. Some research has even shown that simply asking a customer whether they've visited the shop before, instead of whether they need help, can increase retail sales significantly.[10]

The reason questions matter is simple: they allow you to unearth your customer's true needs, rather than the ones you (or they!) think they have, and so increase the probability of a sale. Questions help you understand the root causes of your customer's problems, the impact those problems have on their lives, and their motivators.

Better yet, they can help you understand how your customers feel about their present and future states. Questions, in other words, help you identify and confirm the size of the gap that represents your sales opportunity.

How, though, do you approach this investigation stage in practice? Sales expert Neil Rackham identified four types of question you can ask that can be remembered with a simple mnemonic: SPIN. *Situation, problem, implications* and *need-payoff.*[11]

We start with the *situation* questions to gather general background information that might be helpful – a little about the person we're speaking with, their role and the company. We don't want to spend too much time on these because there is relatively little value to the buyer in explaining this stuff to us. Instead, we want to uncover their needs by probing them with *problem* questions.

There are four things we're trying to get a handle on with problem questions: our customer's ideal future state, the obstacles they must overcome to get to this future state, the root causes of those challenges, and how they feel about it all.

Going back to a point from the beginning of the chapter, making a purchase always involves change, and change tends to provoke an emotional response. So it's important to be clear on what or who is driving the need to solve these problems, and how the customer feels about them. Uncovering these emotive and motivational aspects of the problem space can help us empathise with the customer.

There is no magic formula for asking these questions. The key is to be curious, to listen carefully and, whenever we hit on a potential challenge, to ask them for more detail if it's not quite clear what shape that challenge takes. We can also use our unique insights and the problems we know we can solve for customers to stimulate the discussion.

To provide some examples, a question that helps clarify the desired future state is simply to ask, 'If you solved these problems, how would things be different?' Another couple of questions I often ask as conversations progress are 'What matters most to you about this project?' and 'What matters most to you about who you partner with on this?' The answers are seldom the ones I expect. Better still, prospects often point out that I'm the only person who has ever asked them. The magic, however, is not simply to discover our customer's problems. It's to help them see the *implications*.

People do not spend money or expend effort to solve trivial problems. So if the gap looks small, or the benefits do not obviously outweigh the costs, the hassle of switching to someone else won't seem worthwhile. The genius of asking good 'implication' questions is that they reveal to the customer the true impact of any problems they might be experiencing. One recent discovery call I made, for example, revealed that a prospective client wanted to redesign their product, but didn't have the time or capacity to consolidate their insights and strategic goals into a clear brief for their partners.

What are the implications of this particular problem? In the best case, if the brief is unclear, the partners involved would waste valuable time asking questions they should already have answers to, which would delay the project. In the worst case, if the brief is ambiguous and the team is not aligned, it could compromise the design of the solution, requiring costly rework, or jeopardise the success of the product entirely. Seen in this light, the brief wasn't just a document the boss was too busy to write – the future of the business depended upon it.

Pointing out these implications can transform the customer's perception of the value you might bring, create a greater sense of urgency and increase the likelihood of a sale. This can be an uncomfortable experience for the buyer, however, so to end on a high, you must shift from sad implication questions to happy *need-payoff* questions, which encourage the customer to envisage the solution to their problems and how they stand to benefit – both of which increase their enthusiasm for the purchase.

Need-payoff questions from the example above might include, 'How much of your time will be freed up if somebody helps you write the brief?'; 'If we can produce a better brief in less time, how much would this improve your time-to-market?'; 'How much time do you think a clear brief would save your partners, and what are the associated financial benefits?' Through answering these need-payoff questions, the value you can bring becomes abundantly clear, and the customer will be far more receptive to your proposed solution – assuming you present it well.

Presenting

Presenting your solution will usually involve a written proposal, pitch presentation, demonstration, or all three. The great news is that by this point you should already have a thorough understanding of the customer's problems, they should agree that those problems exist, and they should want to resolve them.

But if you can't explain your solution effectively – as well as provide your prospect with the materials they need to sell the idea internally – you're still not likely to secure commitment. The way you communicate your ideas is vital. The following simple guidelines can have a transformative impact on your written and presentation skills.

Start with the structure

When learning a new skill, we'll find that there are often 'entry tricks' – simple techniques that instantly transform our ability.[12] In photography, for example, there is the *rule of thirds*. Placing the most important visual element of the image a third of the way in from the frame – like the eyes for a portrait or horizon line for a landscape – immediately makes the composition more appealing.

When it comes to producing documents and presentations, there are similar tricks that tackle the single biggest weakness in most documents and presentations: poor structure.

I cannot tell you how many proposals, papers and books I've read, and presentations I've sat through, where I have struggled to absorb the contents because the information is haphazardly presented. Even brilliant ideas are impossible to digest and retain when they're jumbled together. Two structural tricks are particularly useful for avoiding this: the *SCQA Introduction* and the *pyramid principle*.

The SCQA Introduction

The introduction to your document or presentation plays a crucial role in setting the stage for the reader. A well-written introduction compels them to keep reading. A poorly written one switches them off immediately. This is where SCQA comes in: *situation, complications, questions, answers.*[13]

The *situation* comes first. The aim here is to get your readers standing at the same point and looking in the same direction by establishing some basic truths or agreeable remarks about the present. If you're writing a business proposal, for example, you might simply describe the client's ambitions in a sentence or two. If you're writing a pitch deck, your situation might just be an anchoring statement that gets the audience in the correct frame of mind. You've nailed the situation if your reader is nodding along.

Now that you've grounded your audience in the facts of the present, move on to the *complications* – the obstacles, problems or sources of dissatisfaction that are inherent in that situation. These complications hook the reader. They should also already be clear – they are the problems, root causes and implications that were uncovered during your investigation. You've skewered the complications wonderfully if they stop nodding and their brows start to furrow.

The great thing about having outlined the situation and complications is that they naturally raise *questions* in the reader's mind. So now you want to note down what those questions are. There are two reasons for this. First, you might want to explicitly spell them out in your introduction. This has the effect of reassuring the reader that they've understood exactly where you're going, and may even make them feel a little clever that they'd anticipated what's coming next. Second, and more importantly, you must identify those questions because the rest of your document provides the *answers*.

Here's a real-world example I wrote recently that demonstrates this format in action:

[Situation:] Customer experience has become a hot topic in business over the last few years. Customers are in control, we're told. We need to delight them or they'll destroy us. It's no surprise then that businesses the world over have become obsessed with the notion of customer-centricity. They've created customer experience teams and endowed them with generous budgets. Some have even appointed Chief Customer Officers.

[Complications:] Yet few of these initiatives are leading to improvements customers notice, and even fewer producing tangible business results. Demonstrating clear performance improvements remains a major challenge.

[Questions:] This raises two crucial questions for customer experience professionals and the organisations that fund their initiatives. First, how can we make improvements that change the customer's perception of value for the better? And second, how can we do this in a way that makes money?

[Segue to answers:] In this presentation, we'll answer both of these questions in detail. Starting with the bigger challenge – creating a demonstrable payoff for customer experience initiatives.

This short and simple introduction is easy to follow, and the benefits to the reader are immediately apparent. If they want to know the answers to those questions they will likely read on or pay attention to the rest of the presentation.

Now it's time to present your answers, which is where the *pyramid principle* comes into play.

The pyramid principle

The brain finds it easiest to process information that is presented in a clear hierarchy, hence the name – *the pyramid principle*.[14] So when it comes to presenting the meat of your report, proposal or presentation, you must simply group the contents by theme, present the highest-level groupings first, then step down the hierarchy to reveal more information.

For example, I might write: *The most popular pets in suburban Oslo are cats and dogs. Examples of popular dogs include Labradors, German Shepherds and Pomeranians. Examples of popular cats include the Maine Coon, Siamese and Norwegian Forest Cat.*

The chances are that as you reached the end of the second sentence – examples of dogs – you had already anticipated that examples of cats were coming next. That's the power of the pyramid principle. It uses a logical structure, combined with progressive disclosure of detail, to make sure the reader never feels lost in the prose.

The contents of this chapter itself offer another example of the pyramid structure at work. At the top of the pyramid is sales, which is then presented as an end-to-end sales process – prospecting, investigating, presenting and negotiating – the second level of the pyramid. Then I've addressed each in turn, revealing a series of practical sub-points for each key topic – the third level. But how do we know what our pyramid should look like in the first place? The key is to realise that structuring and writing a document or presentation are *separate tasks*.

To the left of my writing desk is a large blank wall where every book, chapter, report, proposal or presentation starts life. I begin by scribbling topics on individual Post-it notes, then look for patterns among them. Over time, logical groupings present themselves, and then, with the complete outline in place, I'm ready to begin writing.

This may sound like extra work, but in fact it is a time-saver, and the larger the document or presentation, the more time it saves. Too often people jump straight into writing, only to get halfway through their work and realise that the whole thing has become a labyrinthine mess and they must start again. This is why publishers typically insist on a thorough proposal and chapter outline before committing to a book idea. Structure first and write later, then when you do start writing, keep the following guidelines in mind.

Use concrete, vivid language

A loathsome school of formal writing favours abstract nouns, verbs made from sawn-off jargon, and overuse of the passive voice – tricks intended to impart an air of authority, literacy and objectivity. But when a reader reaches for a clear call to action, they grasp only boring, opaque and palliative prose. It is impossible to act on because it says almost nothing. Compare these two sentences:

A. *Reduce the domestic canine malnutrition deficit.*
B. *Feed the hungry dog.*

Version A is exactly the kind of guff many businesspeople write, but it's hardly compelling. Version B is clear, concise and actionable, and radiates confidence as a result. Use concrete, vivid language and your prose is immediately more muscular. Improve it further by making your language distinctive.

It is a sad fact that despite the English language comprising upwards of 170,000 words, most businesses use the same handful of buzzwords to describe themselves: *disruptive, innovative, unique, solution-driven, world-class, market-leading, delivery-focused, customer-centric,* blah blah blah. Your audience is bombarded with these lazy platitudes at every hour and from all quarters. They hear: 'These people are as mediocre as everybody else. You would do well to avoid them.'[15] Don't be afraid to use more colourful language, and be sure to include a narrative element too. Storytelling is a deep-rooted human instinct – it's how we teach and learn. Sweeten your narrative arc with little vignettes, interesting anecdotes and real-world examples to bring your document or presentation to life, making it easier to follow and more memorable – especially if it's also concise.

Prioritise ~~ruthlessly~~

The temptation is always to say too much, pointing out every benefit, including every piece of supporting data and sharing all of your knowledge. But not everything you have to say is equally important. The more you say, the more the message is diluted.

It's easy to overwhelm people with information. As an experienced marketer once said to me, 'If you throw me one orange at a time, I can catch them. If you throw me ten at once, I won't catch any.'[16] Ask yourself which three or four things you want the audience to remember from your document, then focus on hammering those points home. They can always ask for more information – they can't ask for less.

When you do communicate your key points, be concise. Brevity shows respect for your reader's time and allows the essentials to shine. A three-page proposal is more likely to be read than a twenty-page one, and its contents more likely to be absorbed. Tightening up language isn't easy, but it improves with practice – something I do by writing pithy LinkedIn posts to fixed character limits.

Keep in mind that just as structuring and writing are separate activities, writing and editing are also different tasks. Once you have a basic draft, ask yourself, 'Do I need this paragraph?', then 'Do I need this sentence?', then 'Do I need this adjective, adverb, clause or filler?' Better yet, ask a friend who is not attached to the work to slim it down. Google Docs is excellent for this because you can see their edits easily. With practice, you'll be surprised how much tighter your language becomes.

Similarly, if you're presenting slides, keep the visual density low to give the content room to breathe, and organise elements into a visual hierarchy. Think of the front page of a newspaper:

the important stuff is big and at the top; details are small and further down. But more important than producing a beautiful presentation is to rehearse.

Rehearse, rehearse, rehearse

A presentation or product demonstration is a performance, and as with any other performance, you have to practise if you're going to do the best job you can. Musicians rehearse. Actors learn their lines. Athletes train. Yet for some reason, people habitually make sales presentations or deliver keynote speeches having never run through them beforehand. Respect your audience and increase your own chances of success – you will never give your best presentation unless you rehearse. It's as simple as that.

Start by running through your presentation alone, reminding yourself that these early attempts are the hardest (and worst) they will ever be. Gradually refine your delivery until timings are consistent and predictable, and you've memorised the key points and their sequence. I cannot overemphasise the value of repetition. Don't think that you can use a script as a shortcut – content is best delivered naturally. You just need to put in the time, and you'll stun the audience with your smooth delivery.

Negotiating

By this point in the sales process you've discovered a prospect, identified their needs through the investigation, and presented a solution. Now you're into the final stage of the funnel: negotiating the terms of the deal.

The most crucial takeaway on this topic is, as with prospecting, that you simply have to do it. Negotiation cannot be avoided – it occurs every time somebody wants something from somebody else – and it can dramatically affect our out-comes. Here are a couple of examples that illustrate the point.

Imagine you've received a job offer and you ask for an extra $10,000 a year, and an additional week's paid leave over and above what is on offer. If they accept your request, over the next five years you'll have made an extra $50,000 – enough to buy a nice new car, pay off a chunk of the mortgage, or mean-ingfully top up your savings, while also enjoying over *a month* more time off.

Perhaps a better example is to consider just how much pri-cing impacts profit. For simplicity's sake, imagine you run a consultancy business that charges $300 per hour and has a 33.3 per cent margin. For every hour you bill, you make $100. Now let's imagine that a customer asks for a $50 discount to $250 per hour. You're eager to win the business so you agree imme-diately with no negotiation. What impact will this have on your profit? It cuts it in half! If they're delighted with your work and keep three of your people busy for a year, you've lost almost a quarter of a million dollars of profit at the stroke of a pen (more on this in Chapter 7). How, then, can you improve your nego-tiation skills? The following tips can help.

Determine your breakpoints

In any negotiation it's important to identify your *breakpoints* – the limit of what you find acceptable for each aspect of the arrangement. When you've defined these points, it is essen-tial to walk away if the line is crossed. Nothing will undermine your position quite like issuing an ultimatum, only to contra-dict yourself and propose your final, final, final offer.

Remember this: *no deal is better than a bad deal.*[17] Don't allow a short-term feeling of accomplishment to set the stage for a long-term disaster. Remember, too, that you can't sell to everyone – it's always a numbers game. There's no need to be afraid of saying no, or hearing it for that matter.

No is good

As counter-intuitive as it sounds, expert negotiators love hearing 'no' for three reasons.

First, as we explored in Chapter 1, people have an innate need to feel in control. So when you give people the right to say no from the outset they immediately feel more at ease and enter a more collaborative frame of mind.

Second, establishing what people definitely *don't* want removes some uncertainty and sets the stage for identifying what they will find acceptable. Many experts see 'no' as the beginning of the negotiation, and attempt to get there early in the dialogue, which brings me on to the third point: 'no' is often the gateway to 'yes'.

Rather than thinking of a no as a flat-out rejection and the end of the discussion, see it as an opportunity to probe further and better discover the other party's needs. 'No' can mean many things: that they're not ready, they need to mull it over, they'd like to do some research, or that you've crossed one of their breakpoints. The only way to find out what it really means is to ask, *What don't you like about our proposal? What would make it acceptable to you?* You may be surprised at how a no can transform into a yes with some thoughtful questioning.

Be conscious of anchoring

Anchoring is a cognitive bias whereby an initial piece of information distorts our perspective or judgement. Unusual examples abound. In 1970, for example, psychologists Kahneman and Tversky ran a two-part experiment. First, participants spun a wheel of fortune with numbers from one to a hundred that was rigged to land on either ten or sixty. Then, they were asked to guess what percentage of African nations were part of the UN. Those whose wheel of fortune landed on a ten guessed around twenty-five per cent. Those whose wheel landed on sixty, however, guessed much higher – forty-five per cent.[18]

As ridiculous as it sounds, our brains struggle to overcome this anchoring effect. We subconsciously use the first value we hear – the anchor – as a starting point that we adjust to arrive at our final answer, a tendency that has serious implications when it comes to negotiation.

If the other party goes first, they may set an anchor that distorts our judgement of what terms we should accept. In fact, initial proposals are often deliberately exaggerated in the hope that by the time negotiations are settled, the end result is more palatable. So what should you do about it?

Instead of getting wound up by outlandish suggestions, you must simply do your best to recognise the anchoring effect at work, and calmly propose something else. The alternative is to go first yourself, in which case it's you who sets the anchor, which brings me neatly on to my next tip.[19]

Be ambitious (without being ridiculous)

Given the anchoring effect, it is unsurprising that those who ask for more tend to get more. Yet many of us do the opposite. Maybe we don't want to appear greedy, are worried what people will think of us, or don't feel confident. The fact is, though, as negotiations expert Natalie Reynolds explains, that if your counter-party immediately accepts your offer, you haven't been ambitious enough. 'I always advise my clients to work out their ambitious opener and then add on another ten per cent, just to counter the tendency most of us have to misjudge what we really mean by ambitious,' she writes.[20]

This may all seem a little unnecessary. Why can't we just offer something fair and avoid all this silly back and forth? The short answer is that fairness is a matter of perception – a lesson I learned the hard way when I began my speaking career.

When my first book came out, it wasn't long before I started getting enquiries about speaking. I was grateful for the opportunities and set a price that I thought was fair for a beginner – £2,000 for a turn at the podium. Clients were delighted and I had plenty of work.

Then one day I had an offer to speak in Germany. The organiser was similarly keen on agreeing a fair price, so set one for me. 'There will be no negotiation,' he said. 'The fee will be fifteen thousand.' I was shocked.

To check whether this was an extreme outlier, the next day I called a previous client and asked how much they'd budgeted for me to speak. 'Oh yeah – we were delighted with your quote! We'd set aside twenty thousand as we did with all the other speakers at the event. In fact, you should probably raise your prices.'

Suddenly my figure didn't seem fair at all. As I mentally added up how much money I'd left on the table over the last three years, I learned my lesson well: what's fair is a matter of opinion. There is no downside to being ambitious. The worst they can say is no, which could still lead to a better yes.

Keep the whole in mind

Most negotiations are multidimensional. In a typical business contract they might involve the price, the payment terms, the ownership of intellectual property, whether the deal can be used in PR campaigns, the scope of work, and who will be responsible for what.

With this in mind, the key to a successful negotiation is to aim for total value and see all the component parts of the deal as interconnected. You might agree to maintain your price but accept longer payment terms, or meet a crucial timeline but with a reduced scope of work. Either way, the magic phrase to use in business negotiations, according to Reynolds, is, '*If you . . . then I . . .*'. The aim is to construct mutually beneficial trade-offs that create the most value for everyone.[21]

Negotiation guru Chris Voss develops this concept further still, suggesting you co-opt your counter-party by asking them open-ended questions – especially 'How' questions, which are seen as requests for help. For example, if the opposite party suggests that you accept ninety-day payment terms, you might say, 'How am I supposed to do that when our upfront investment is so substantial, and our suppliers demand payment in advance?' Phrased this way, you perform a kind of mental aikido move – transforming an unpalatable suggestion on their part into a collaborative problem-solving exercise, which is exactly how you should approach every negotiation.[22]

Try to agree, rather than to win

Negotiation experts quibble a little over some tactics. Some think it's best to go first, others that it's best to wait for the other party to reveal their hand. Some put greater emphasis on upfront planning, others on how dynamic and uncertain negotiations can be. Yet one area of near-unanimous agreement is that the aim of negotiations is not to 'win' – you must not regard the other party as an enemy or adversary to be beaten.

As Voss explains, 'The person across the table is never the problem. The unsolved issue is. So focus on the issue. This is one of the most basic tactics for avoiding emotional escalations . . . [T]he adversary is the situation . . . [and] the person that you appear to be in conflict with is actually your partner.'[23]

Keep in mind that, in business, the end of a negotiation is often the beginning of a working relationship, so it's better to start off on a good footing, having demonstrated an ability to work effectively as a team – just one of the topics addressed in Part Three, which explains how best to launch, grow, manage and lead a business in our uncertain world.

Chapter summary

- Selling involves identifying the gap between where a customer is today – their *current state* – and where they want to be – their *future state*.
- The sales process involves four phases: prospecting, investigating, presenting and negotiating.
- Prospecting is an essential activity and a numbers game. If you don't keep putting more prospects in the top of your funnel, your pipeline will dry up and growth will stall.
- Prepare for prospecting by developing a target customer profile based on problems you know you can help solve.
- Be clear on a compelling reason why the customer should buy from you.
- Top salespeople are not afraid to challenge their customers with new insights that make them think, or to question their customers' assumptions and beliefs.

- Use social media to build familiarity which will make the prospecting process easier.
- Investigation – discovering the customer's true needs – involves two skills: listening and asking the right questions.
- The questions you should ask during the investigation phase can be remembered with a simple mnemonic, SPIN: *situation, problem, implications* and *need-payoff*.
- The biggest weakness in most written documents and presentations is poor structure.
- You can improve the way you introduce your ideas by using the SCQA format: situation, complications, questions, answers.
- Using the pyramid principle will help you arrange your ideas into a logical form.
- Rehearsing is vital for any presentation – do not skip it!
- Remember that no deal is better than a bad deal and define the breakpoints at which you will walk away.
- Don't be afraid of 'no' in a negotiation. It is often the gateway to 'yes'.
- Be conscious of how anchoring effects can distort your judgement and don't be afraid to put forward your proposal first.
- Open ambitiously – the more you ask for, the more you're likely to get.
- When negotiating, keep the whole package in mind and take a collaborative approach rather than trying to win.

Part 3

Launching, growing and managing organisations that thrive on uncertainty

6 Starting up

Managing the perilous uncertainties of entrepreneurship

No aspect of business is as fraught with uncertainty as bringing a new venture, product or service to market. *Will customers love our idea? How will rivals respond? How much are people willing to pay?* We can never be sure in advance.

Add on a host of other factors that must come together in symphonic harmony – production costs, legal compliance, promotion, supplier relationships and cash flow – and it's unsurprising that many new ventures splutter then conk out immediately, or must shapeshift several times before they take flight.

How do successful entrepreneurs navigate such extreme uncertainty? Part Two provided many of the answers. Yet in practical terms there is more to explore. Because of the levels of uncertainty involved, the methods entrepreneurs use to bring a new concept to market are a world away from those typically favoured by the mainstream – especially the prevalent practices within larger, more established organisations. How so? Let's explore the most common differences.

Affordable loss vs return on investment

Experienced entrepreneurs know they can't control the future. So instead of setting a desired return on investment, they work on the basis of *affordable loss* – the maximum they're prepared to spend to try their idea out – a concept we've already touched on in previous chapters.[1] They also aim to overcapitalise the business to provide a financial buffer should they need to change direction in response to market feedback. Without this contingency they risk diluting the value of the business in a down round – raising more funds at a lower valuation.

In contrast, mainstream management practices require projects to have business cases that focus on the anticipated returns on investment, even though in most situations such payoffs cannot be forecast accurately. As a consequence, numbers can be fudged to make just about any project seem enticing, and sponsors throw good money after bad when results fall short. Part of the problem is that figures and calculations provide such a potent illusion of certainty. We have a hard time realising that numbers *are not facts* – that we can write fiction as easily in Excel as in Word or PowerPoint – and are seduced into making unnecessarily risky decisions.

What's the alternative? Instead of wasting time on complex return-on-investment calculations that skew your focus towards possible upsides, reframe your decision-making with the aim of *controlling your downside*.

The key question to ask is not 'How much will it cost me to design, build and launch A, B or C?' or 'What kind of payback will I get if I invest X?' It is 'How much can I afford to spend to find out if this idea might work?'

When we work from this basis of affordable loss, the worst possible outcome is that we spend a reasonable amount of time and money learning about something – not that we commit to a prospective catastrophe.

Market orientated vs organisation orientated

If you work in a large organisation, the chances are that you'll have heard countless remarks like the following, dredged from my memories of projects past:

'Customers are complaining about how complex this process is. They want it to be simpler – just like it is with our competitors – but our systems don't allow it, so that's that.'

'User research informed the ideal navigation structure for the site, but our VPs think their divisions should each have a button on the main nav, so that's what we're designing.'

'The CEO really wants this feature, so we've moved it to the top of the priority list over the stuff our users have been urgently requesting.'

These Dilbertesque disclosures have a common denominator: the actions suit the organisation in the short term, rather than satisfy what the market – customers, competitors and industry dynamics – is demanding of them to thrive in the future. Product-market fit has been ignored in favour of product-organisation fit.

There are any number of reasons why these counterproductive behaviours happen. Large organisations are social structures, so politics is unavoidable. Then there's the golden rule – *the person with the gold rules* – so budget-holders have the final say over what gets done. Success brings laxity, and complacency too – a phenomenon known as 'victory disease' – which encourages organisation-led decision-making.

There's also the issue of *skin in the game*. If employees face no significant upside or downside as a result of their successes or failures, they have little incentive to make market-oriented decisions. Founders, small business owners and entrepreneurs, by contrast, experience these risks and rewards every day, which explains their fixation on the market.

I've yet to meet a successful entrepreneur or founder who didn't show a near-obsessive interest in what is going on *out there*. They are intensely curious about the problems they can solve, the needs they can meet, and they thrive on feedback – often treating early customers like partners who can help shape the product itself. They also want to understand and evaluate the alternatives customers would consider, and how they can outperform them.

This is not to say that they delegate responsibility for their vision or product design to their customers, immediately gratify their every whim, or become fixated on their rivals. Rather, they know their assumptions might be wrong, others may not share their vision, or there might be opportunities to create more value, increase engagement or sell more.

As intelligence officer turned novelist John Le Carré once wrote: 'A desk is a dangerous place from which to view the world.'[2] Instead, we must build *psychological proximity* – immersing ourselves in the customer's world and seeing it through their eyes. Something each of us can do with a little effort, regardless of how big or small our venture.

In some large companies, for example, senior executives spend a proportion of their time on the shop floor or manning a phone in the contact centre. Others go a step further, encouraging their staff to have the same first-hand experience as customers. When engineer Yuji Yokoya was tasked with improving the Toyota Sienna, for example, he hopped in one and drove 53,000 miles across America. In the course of his journey, he spotted a whole host of opportunities to make the family wagon more child- and driver-friendly.

We can also interact with customers and prospects directly, rather than relying on dashboards or metrics to guide our decision-making – something many founders and entrepreneurs do instinctively. Jim Jannard, the founder of Oakley and Red Digital Cinema, spent hours chatting with customers on their user forum as the company grew.[3] All of which brings us on to another crucial point: entrepreneurs are fundamentally concerned with the real world.

Works in practice vs works on paper

In Chapter 1 we reached a simple yet profound conclusion: that the world is inherently unpredictable. People don't always do what they say or know what they want. We can't get perfect information to make perfect decisions, and even if we have the right theory or strategy, much of our success depends on execution.

The only thing that matters, then, is what works in practice, not what works on paper. It is not possible to analyse our way into certain success; we need to try things out and see what happens. And this focus on the real world – rather than the hypothetical, theoretical and analytical – underpins a host of further differences between entrepreneurial methods and the typical management practices of larger, more established businesses. Here are three such examples.

Start selling earlier

A surprising trait among expert entrepreneurs is how early they start selling. In fact, they often consider selling and market research to be the same thing.

Because their approach to selling is consultative – they are uncovering the customer's needs using the processes we described in the previous chapter – it constitutes a powerful form of research that gives them insights that help shape the product from day one.

Many entrepreneurs begin selling before the product even exists, launching crowdfunding campaigns to see if people back their ideas, or using mockups to run adverts on social media and see whether people click through or register their interest.[4] Tesla – a famously entrepreneurial company – do something similar with their new cars, making them available for pre-order before they are manufactured. Their success challenges the notion that such methods are impractical in many categories.

The approach typically taken by less experienced founders, or managers within larger businesses, could hardly be more different. They perform detached, logical analyses of the market, often using off-the-shelf reports available to everyone in the industry, rather than getting out of the office and into the field. Where qualitative research is conducted it's usually kept to a bare minimum – perhaps a handful of interviews with prospects just to say it was done – and attempts at selling don't begin until the product is launched.

It's not hard to see why such an approach can end in tears. If the initial vision is wrong, and there is no genuine means to course-correct as the project progresses, the business development team is often left trying to sell a product nobody wants.

What else, besides trying to sell the product earlier, can we do to avoid these risks? One solution is to focus on building a real, working prototype as early as possible.

Build real stuff

It's easy for months to go by as we write detailed business cases and elaborate project plans. But entrepreneurs and successful startup founders don't really go in for these kinds of things. They know that *show me* beats *tell me*, that it doesn't matter how promising a technological innovation might be if we can't get it to work, and that the sooner they get something real into people's hands the more valuable their feedback will be.

That's why Marc Benioff, the founder of Salesforce, invited as many people as possible to the apartment where he founded the company to test-drive prototypes.[5] Similarly, Michael Bloomberg would take cups of coffee into an investment bank, offering them to anyone who'd give him feedback on his product idea in the early days.[6]

Another advantage of creating a functional prototype is that often you don't really know what you're building, or what makes it good, until after you've made it. The prototyping process itself is a means to answer unanswered questions, narrow the scope as unforeseen costs and complexities emerge, and communicate our assumptions to both our team and prospective customers.

This approach can work just as well in a large corporation as in a startup, and can even be conducted in total secrecy, as the development process for the iPhone illustrates. When the product and user interface were being developed, every idea began life as a working demonstration, which then progressed through successive rounds of feedback.

First, the immediate team would review the demo and suggest improvements, then the next level of management would review it too. Eventually, once demos were deemed good enough, they would make their way up to Steve Jobs, who would give the final approval.

By following this process – described as *creative selection* by engineer Ken Kocienda who worked there at the time – a working version of each feature was evaluated by a large group of critical thinkers who formed an acceptable proxy for the real customer base.[7] It's an approach all too rarely tried elsewhere. Many organisations regard user testing as a cursory check before launch to tick a box, not the driver of *what the project should be.*

The lesson is simple. There is no acceptable substitute for reality. You need to build real stuff to test your ideas. Start with a crude prototype, then use feedback from your network, subject matter experts and early customers to refine it, until an acceptable first version is market-ready.

Confirm by experience

Savvy entrepreneurs know not to double down on a new venture until there are confirmatory signs from the market that what the entrepreneurs see as an opportunity is also a viable concern, and they will often make the hard choice to pull the plug even very late in the game.

James Dyson – Britain's richest man at the time of writing – abandoned his attempt to enter the electric car market after spending half a billion pounds of his own money, when it became clear that the venture was not commercially viable.[8] Had he persisted in the face of such evidence, losses could have been huge. And to that extent, the reason he has generated such spectacular wealth for himself over the years is *because* of his willingness to say no when there are concerns about viability, not *in spite of it*.

What kind of confirmatory evidence are we talking about? If we've started selling early we'll have some idea of whether prospective customers are interested. And if we've focused on building something real we'll also know whether the product works effectively and should have a clear idea of whether production can be scaled at reasonable cost. We may even have some early adopter customers whose feedback can help inform our judgement.

By contrast, executives within large organisations often commit wholeheartedly to a project based on little more than some unproven hypotheses and eye candy in a PowerPoint presentation. Projects are given the green light and budgets to proceed, only to detonate on impact with the market. And since without an active project employees don't have any work to do (and their consulting partners can't charge for their services), they're often unwittingly incentivised to keep projects alive, even if they're a total boondoggle.

The most wasteful thing we can do, though, is not to sit idle, but *to labour on the wrong product*, since the end result is a failed project with far greater losses than necessary, especially if we insist on sticking to the plan.

Learn and adapt vs stick to the plan

When my business partner Ben and I decided to launch what would become Methodical – the design agency we run together today – we began by taking a four-day retreat in rural Belgium where we could hatch our master plan in peace. In retrospect, our pontificating and Post-it noting were all but a total waste of time.

Within a year of launching the business, the only two aspects of our plan still in place were our commitment to partner together, and a cost structure that favoured lower fixed costs and higher variable costs to keep our nascent enterprise adaptable.

And adapt we did. We even changed the name of the business, along with how it made money. The planning may have been valuable, but the plan certainly wasn't. It was just our best guess of what we thought might work.

Successful entrepreneurs are similarly aware that their assumptions about any aspect of their venture could easily be wrong, so they see the initial vision as a hypothesis to be tested, shaped and refined, not as *an irreversible commitment.*[9] Adobe's original business plan, for example, was to build computers, laser printers and typesetting equipment bundled with software – an idea they used to raise $2.5 million in funding. But prospective customers weren't interested. They already had computers and deals with other brands to supply printers. What they really needed was the software that allowed the computers and printers to work together. Meeting this need necessitated a fundamental change to Adobe's business plan, but it was one that subsequently propelled the company to great success.[10]

Such manoeuvres are comparatively rare in large corporations. Instead, the initial plan tends to be executed as-is, even in the face of incontrovertible evidence that it's flawed – a pattern that has played out so many times over the course of my career that it seems almost law-like. In fact, as I sit here racking my brains, I can think of only two companies I've worked with in the last decade that have abandoned or significantly altered a product plan in response to research conducted as the project progressed.

Remember: opportunities are not hidden jewels buried in the market, waiting to be unearthed; they are fabricated from what we know, who we know and the materials we have at our collective disposal. As these resources come together, elements of the vision, product, service and business model gradually take shape.

Often, for example, a startup team comes together before they have any vision for a product at all. And even when they do have an idea, it can change quite radically before it finally sees the light of day. The founders of Shazam were keen to work together, but couldn't decide whether to sell contact lenses online, or launch an app that recognises the music that's playing on the radio.[11]

When entrepreneurs do have a vision for a product, their first port of call is usually other experts – investors, domain specialists, prospective customers or partners – whose feedback is the first step to validating the idea, and whose commitment, if they're interested, helps shape its direction.

In this way the startup team self-selects into a committed group of experts who are more likely to work as an effective team – moulding the idea together like wet clay. This is in stark contrast to working practices within some large organisations, who often start with a vision cooked up in a workshop, then assign a group of individuals to bring it to market, regardless of whether or not they buy into the idea.

This raises a crucial question. When we do have an idea for a new business, product or service, how do we know whether it is likely to succeed? Here, again, seasoned entrepreneurs have much to teach us. Essentially, their approach to evaluating or targeting their products differs from those of the management of mainstream organisations in three fundamental ways: they care more about timing than features, focus more on creating value than being unique, and seek to change the game rather than play by the existing rules.

The right time vs the right features

Expert entrepreneurs are aware of a simple truth: if the timing is wrong, everything is wrong. Before they fuss over the details of their product, they therefore determine whether this is the right moment to launch it – whether they can ride a wave of change, take advantage of a macro trend, a technology reaching critical mass, or some other tipping point. Only then will they consider what the product and business model could be.

This preoccupation with timing comes across in the most compelling startup pitches and sales narratives. These, as expert Andy Raskin explains, tend to follow a consistent structure. Their authors start by naming a major change in the world that brings with it high stakes and urgency for the prospective customer or investor. Next, they show that this change will create winners and losers – that taking advantage of it will create opportunity, while resistance will be catastrophic.

Third, they 'tease the promised land' by showing what success looks like in this new world (a similar idea to the *future state* I discussed in the previous chapter). And finally, with the audience foaming with excitement, they reveal how their product or service is the key to the kingdom, supporting their pitch with some real-world evidence.[12] The whole narrative is built around *the change in the world* and why *now is the time*.

Established brands, by contrast, almost never consider timing as the primary determinant of success. Instead, they tend to believe that once they have decided to enter a market they can spend their way to victory. For them, timing is about launch planning, project deadlines and pinpointing which features can be achieved. They're not the only sinners in this regard. Many first-time founders and entrepreneurs are so entranced with their concept that they do not stop to wonder whether the timing is right.

Of course, there's no magic formula that reveals exactly when you should launch. Timing is one of the uncertainties in our environment that cannot be completely analysed out. But you can seek to align your ideas with discernible macro trends: a critical threshold of technology adoption, say, or a major socio-economic shift; a favourable change in regulations or a massive increase in demand within your category or an adjacent one.

One of our clients, for example, has developed a highly effective non-drug treatment for Generalised Anxiety Disorder. In my view, the timing is perfect. It's clear that, for various reasons (economic pressures and the Covid pandemic among them), anxiety has been on the increase in recent years. It's also apparent that the stigma attached to it is declining and that people are therefore more likely to feel comfortable seeking help. At the same time, concern about the side effects of prescription medications for anxiety and depression – addiction, weight gain and sexual dysfunction among them – have made their way into public discourse. It seems the right time for a non-drug treatment for a major health issue to make its appearance.

Another example from Csaba's portfolio of startups is Hum Capital – a platform designed to make it easier for businesses to raise funding by matching them to suitable lenders or investors. Why is the timing right for Hum as a concept? Because a crucial threshold of businesses now use cloud-based accounting and payment systems, which can share data with their platform.

As these two examples make clear, the vital question to ask

yourself when embarking on any new venture, then, is not 'Why this product?' but 'Why this product *now*?'

Simply better vs unique selling point

Another mistake people commonly make during the product development stage is to focus on creating something with a *unique selling point*. What we should be focusing on instead is creating products that *satisfy our customer's fundamental needs in a better way.*

For every product or service category there are basic sources of value that matter to most buyers most of the time. For example, every e-commerce shopper wants prompt, reliable delivery, hassle-free returns and an easy check-out process. Unique features or selling points – by virtue of the fact that they are *not* generic category benefits – matter far less, far less often, and to a smaller number of customers. Comparatively few shoppers, for instance, will choose an online service solely on the grounds that it can, say, split packages in a single order across multiple delivery addresses.

In our uncertain world, where success is largely a numbers game, a product that appeals to more people in more circumstances is more likely to succeed than one that is simply different. In fact, some would go so far as to say the target market for any product should be all the buyers within a given category. These observations raise two important questions.

First, aren't these basic sources of value just table stakes? Doesn't everyone have to provide them? Yes. But performance on the most fundamental elements of a product or service is typically so variable between brands that it dominates all other considerations among buyers, so should be the primary focus.[13]

Second, don't we need to stand out or offer some clear

reason for customers to choose us over alternatives? Again, yes. But the way we do that is to focus on what provides the most value to the customer, rather than focusing on creating something unique. Better is almost always different, but different isn't always better, and we can always make our product stand out further through creative, distinctive advertising and promotion.[14]

When planning a new venture, then, it's worth spending time to discover what really matters most to buyers, and whether you can noticeably outperform the alternatives in at least one of those areas. If you can't, clever unique features will be for nothing. Ask yourself, 'What does simply better look like to our customers?' Focus most of your attention on those fundamental sources of value – whether it's a lower price point, better quality, a particular set of features and functions, or all three.

Game changers vs game players

We can think of businesses as falling into one of two camps. The first plays according to the rules of the game as they are broadly understood today; the second changes the rules or invents a new game altogether.

The former conforms to the consensus – the established way of doing things. The latter defies consensus with some kind of twist in the business: a different operating, marketing or revenue model, the development of new technologies, or perhaps the form or function of the product itself. You can tell if a business idea defies consensus because it's never been tried before, polarises opinion, deviates from existing practices, or all of the above.

Red Bull is a good example. Not only does it taste odd, it

comes in a tiny can, and contains taurine – an amino acid found in meat and fish. It sounds like an unlikely winner when you put it like that, but Red Bull created a global energy drinks brand and sells over 7.5 billion cans a year.[15] Crocs are another good example. Some people love them, others hate them, but these comfort-first plastic clogs are undeniably successful, with over 600 million pairs sold to date.[16]

Then there's Salesforce. While we take the software-as-a-service model for granted today, it was by no means a given that their enterprise platform would succeed. And while the iPod and iPhone went on to become huge successes, when they were launched there was no shortage of scepticism. What is a computer company doing making a personal music player? Who would pay hundreds of dollars for a phone that doesn't have a keyboard? Microsoft CEO Steve Ballmer found the iPhone so fanciful he famously laughed at the price and lack of business-friendly functionality.[17]

Why does it matter? Because while these elements of non-consensus bring greater risk to the venture, they are also what create the potential for outsized payoffs. If everything we do is logical, obvious and well-understood, there is no potential for disproportionate rewards because there can be no advantages – intellectual property, inimitable aspects or innovations – that deliver beyond-average value to customers or investors.

As venture capitalist Paul Graham explains, 'There are some kinds of work that you can't do well without thinking differently from your peers. To be a successful scientist, for example, it's not enough just to be correct. Your ideas have to be both correct and novel. You can't publish papers saying things other people already know. You need to say things no one else has realised yet.

'You see this pattern with startup founders, too. You don't

want to do something that everyone agrees is a good idea, or there will already be other companies doing it. You have to do something that sounds to most other people like a bad idea, but that you know isn't.'[18]

That's not to say you can't make a good living running a consensus business – in fact, almost every business that starts out defying the consensus becomes the new model to emulate if they achieve great success. And there are plenty of great village florists, bike shops, boutique design agencies and restaurants that successfully follow tried-and-true business models and propositions – it's just that they can't offer outsized returns.

The problem for most large, traditionally run businesses is that they want to create hot new products but they approach them as consensus businesses, not as entrepreneurs. They tend to believe that conforming to the status quo is a good thing because their current success *is the status quo*, and their hyper-rational, analytical processes filter out anything contentious.

By wanting to know that they'll succeed before they launch – they've promised a return on investment, after all – they daren't try anything risky, and thus take the biggest risk of all: creating me-too products that serve only to remind their customers of the market leader. In fact, some act like they're the market leader already, and waste time optimising their product before its value is even proven, the last difference we'll address.

Get traction then optimise vs optimise then get traction

When a product or service is your baby, or you're used to working on mature offerings that have benefited from years of efficiency gains, it's natural to want to optimise everything before it goes to market. Whether it's a point of personal pride or force of habit, many of us are hesitant to launch until our offering includes every feature people could want, every process is streamlined and our infrastructure can scale efficiently. In reality, though, optimisation is a waste of time and money if we haven't yet got traction.

That's not to say that the first version of our product or service can be poor – it needs to provide the fundamental source of value that we're promising. Whether that be attractive appearance, ease of use, style, reliability, safety, or something else – it absolutely must have them. As the investor and entrepreneur Scott Belsky explains in his wonderful book *The Messy Middle*, you can't just sprinkle what makes your concept special on top, it needs to be baked in from the start.[19] And when our first customers come along, we must do everything we can to satisfy and impress them.

Yet at the same time we must avoid the temptation to optimise unimportant aspects of our offering before we really need to. Do you really need a sexy logo and website to get started? Probably not, yet this is a primary focus for many in the early days. Do you need complex customer relationship management software when you don't have any customers? Unlikely, yet one startup I worked with fussed over this non-issue endlessly before ultimately finding out that their product was undesirable. Should you scale up manufacturing or distribution infrastructure when you've no idea how the product will sell? Again, probably not. Do you need certain nice-to-have features that few customers will use in the first release? No. It's ok that the first version of a new product isn't perfect, because the first customers aren't expecting perfection.

As Belsky explains, our customers tend to evolve alongside our offering in the following sequence: *willing*, *forgiving*, *viral*, *valuable* then *profitable*.[20] Our first customers are simply those who are willing to try our product or service. We just want a few of them so we can deal with them personally and seek as much feedback as we can. They are more like partners or testers – helping us iron out the kinks. Our next cohort are those who are not the ultra-early adopters, but who are sufficiently enthusiastic to forgive some of the flaws and foibles that come with our early version, and are excited to see how it develops.

From here, assuming all is well, we should have achieved that entrepreneurial miracle: product-market fit. Now it's time to spread the word far and wide, and make sure our customers have an experience with the product that's worth talking about. These viral customers are a vital part of our growth engine, alongside our other promotional activity. Finally, as our product approaches maturity, we want to attract the most valuable customers – those with the greatest possible lifetime value and potential profitability.

Clearly then, at each stage of customer development (as opposed to product or service development), the level and nature of our optimisation activities is different. There's no point in developing ultra-efficient processes to maximise customer profitability if we've not yet found any willing customers, for example. And avoiding the temptation to optimise and scale up prematurely will save you time and money.

No discussion of this topic would be complete without mentioning Webvan – a famous flameout during the dot-com bubble at the turn of the century – whose idea was to home-deliver groceries ordered online (a concept that was ultimately mistimed, but is now commonplace). Critics cite numerous reasons for their colossal failure, but there is seemingly unanimous agreement that the decision to build the company's entire infrastructure from scratch – complete with their own software and distribution centres – was a bad idea when the fundamentals of the value proposition and business model were unproven.[21] Ultimately the venture lost over $800 million before filing for bankruptcy in 2001.

Contrast this with the approach Nick Swinmurn took when a frustrating experience trying to find shoes in the style, size and colour he liked inspired him to launch an online store called shoesite.com. To Swinmurn it didn't make sense to raise money and build complex infrastructure until it was clear his idea had merit. He opted instead to go to shoe shops near his home and ask if he could photograph the shoes they had available. He'd then list them on his simple website, and if someone ordered them he'd go back to the store, buy the shoes and ship them. Once it was clear that the business idea had potential, his next step was to strike deals with some major distributors who would ship the shoes to customers for him.[22] It was only later, as they grew under their new name – Zappos.com – that the business built their own fulfilment centres.

The entrepreneurial process

By now it should be clear that when developing new products, services or businesses, expert entrepreneurs often operate according to a fundamentally different set of principles from those in the management mainstream.

And in comparing these approaches we can see that by promising returns, sticking with their visions, prioritising desk-based research instead of learning from prospective customers, and committing too early, those who attempt to develop new products based solely on logical, detached analysis and seeing a deliberate strategy through can easily come unglued. These methods simply aren't compatible with the inherent uncertainties within the environment. Contrary to popular belief then, successful entrepreneurs are actually quite risk averse, and their corporate counterparts often absurdly reckless in comparison.

So far I've talked about the entrepreneurial approach as a mindset rather than as a process, but there are certain common activities that successful entrepreneurs pursue and that form a sequence. In essence, these are:

1. Noodling with an opportunity
2. Gathering expert feedback
3. Prototyping and primary research
4. Iterative product development
5. Sell, sell, sell

1. Noodling with an opportunity

It all begins with the whiff of opportunity. Inspiration may strike in the shower. Our entrepreneur might be frustrated with a product or service they use as a customer. They could observe a problem in the environment and see opportunity in solving it, or become aware of some new law, technology or other change in the world that opens up an avenue worth exploring.

Someone from their network might share an idea, or they might have a random conversation with a stranger that leads somewhere interesting. They might even just like the idea of working with a friend or two on a new venture. Wherever it comes from, when an idea excites them, the first thing they instinctively do is start noodling around with it.

How would it work? Who is it for? Has anybody already solved this problem? Is now the right time? How large is the addressable market? What are the alternatives?

The culmination of this noodling – if they're sufficiently confident in their idea – is usually some kind of vision statement or pitch deck that allows them to communicate the idea with others. At Amazon, for example, those with new ideas write a fictional press release that describes the product or service as if it had just been launched.[23]

2. Gathering expert feedback

The second activity, which can overlap with the first and subsequent phases, is a truth-seeking exercise: gathering feedback from those whose opinions they think are worth listening to, such as subject matter experts and prospective customers, investors and team members.

They might start, for example, with those who know the particular market well, or with subject matter experts who can advise on the feasibility of the concept. They might also sound out a fellow entrepreneur who is good at playing devil's advocate, or prospective customers whose problems they think they're solving. Whoever they talk to, these people's feedback will give an early sense of the challenges they must overcome, and whether their idea is worth pursuing. Some of those experts may even want to come on board. In fact, the most obvious validation they can hope for early on – before a product or customer even exists – is whether investors are willing to fund an idea should they need it, or whether others are prepared to join their team and work on the concept with them.

When Elon Musk became enthusiastic about space travel, for example, he relocated to Los Angeles where he would be closer to the world's leading experts in aeronautics, and where many of the major industry players did most of their manufacturing and R&D. He also got involved with the Mars Society – a non-profit group that was interested in exploring the red planet – his first step towards building a network of experts he could use as a sounding board, and he began hosting salons where the possibilities could be debated.

As his network expanded he was eventually introduced to Tom Mueller, an industry veteran and expert engineer who was willing and able to help Musk refine his emerging vision for a low-cost rocket. Together they founded Space Exploration Technologies in 2002.[24] Today, SpaceX is famous for the incredible spectacle of their reusable rockets coming in to land, and the business is worth an estimated $74 billion.[25]

3. Prototyping and primary research

If our entrepreneur is still enthusiastic about their idea by this stage, it's time to knuckle down to either testing out the concept with a prototype (especially if it requires technical innovations), conducting more primary research with target customers to uncover their problems, wants and needs, or both.

They can also begin to gauge product-market fit with tentative sales efforts – by demonstrating their prototype and taking deposits for pre-orders, for example; or assessing interest with a basic website and some social media ads to see if people get in touch for more information.

4. Iterative product development

With early signs from the market that they're onto something, or a proof of concept that they believe in, it's time to evolve the prototype into the first proper version of the product. This is typically a highly iterative process of design, development and testing, during which they will continue to solicit real-world feedback and solve problems as they go.

The outcome of this phase will be a major milestone: the product they're taking to market, accompanied by plans for how they intend to advertise, sell and distribute it to early customers – the next phase.

5. Sell, sell, sell

Depending on the product or service in question, and the existing brand presence if it's already an established business, the launch could be a low-key affair – a quiet release to a select group of early adopters who can help further refine the product – or something more impressive, accompanied by advertising campaigns and PR initiatives. The overall aim, though, is to sell the product to real customers.

When Morgan McLachlan, Mark Lynn and Csaba founded Amass – a botanics brand that began by making an artisanal gin – they started by using third-party distilleries to create a product to their specification, experimenting with recipes until they had the taste, aroma and packaging dialled in to their satisfaction. They then hired a single salesperson – an experienced veteran from the drinks industry – to hit the streets and start selling to one bar and restaurant at a time. It was only later on, when the brand had established itself, that they secured nationwide distribution and began to scale up rapidly. There was nothing more complicated to it than that.

As this example neatly captures, in reality there's no great mystique to entrepreneurship. It's hard work, and not for the faint of heart. But that's because creating a new venture, product or service is inherently uncertain and there are many moving parts to contend with, not because the necessary actions are beyond us.

By far the biggest hurdle for most people is to recognise that launching a new business is first and foremost a pragmatic undertaking, not an intellectual contest. If you can get real, you can get results.

Chapter summary

- Because entrepreneurs accept uncertainty as a fact of life, they take a radically different approach to developing new products, services or ventures.
- Expert entrepreneurs test their ideas using *the principle of affordable loss* to limit their downside, rather than setting a desirable return on investment.
- Entrepreneurs are *market orientated*, focusing on the needs of the customer and dynamics of the environment, above what is convenient for their organisation.
- Successful entrepreneurs are also exclusively concerned with what works in practice rather than what works on paper, building real products for real people so they can get real feedback.
- As their projects progress, expert entrepreneurs remain adaptable and focus on learning.
- When it comes to the product itself, successful entrepreneurs typically begin with whether it's fundamentally the right time for the product, not what the feature set should be.
- They also aim to create products that are simply better than the alternatives – offering more value to more buyers more of the time – rather than starting with a unique selling point that only appeals to a small sub-section of the market.

- Successful entrepreneurs are also unafraid of defying consensus – in fact they recognise this as their biggest competitive advantage.
- They also avoid wasting time and money on unnecessary optimisation before launch – waiting until they have traction first.
- Contrary to popular belief, successful entrepreneurs are actually quite risk averse compared to those within the management structures of most large organisations. Their processes are also far simpler and more pragmatic.
- Entrepreneurs tend to start product development by noodling with the opportunity and gathering expert feedback. Next, they build a proof of concept or prototype and conduct as much primary research as possible. If they're convinced the idea has merit, they enter a period of iterative product development, before launching the first version of their product and getting to work on sales and marketing.

7 Growth

The ten paths to growth and how to apply them

Once a new product, service or venture gains traction, our focus naturally shifts to growth. And here at last, one might assume, the tempestuous uncertainty of the early days subsides, and we can rely on good old-fashioned theory, analysis and data to illuminate the path to riches.

Well, sort of.

While there are certain reliable principles that we can employ to help us grow, and a finite number of levers we can pull, the eventual outcomes of any growth plan remain uncertain for a number of reasons.

For starters, we need to know what those reliable principles are and then apply them. The fact is, though, that many of the most effective approaches are not widely understood or run contrary to established management dogma. We also need to identify which of our possible growth levers offer the greatest payoff at a given time and focus our attention on those. But this requires exactly the kind of systems thinking that many organisations struggle with.

It would help, of course, if we had reliable data to hand. But often we do not, and even if we do, we can easily misinterpret what it's telling us. Our challenges don't end there. Applying a proven principle doesn't guarantee results because so much depends on how well the theory is executed. For example, it's one thing to state that we will build our brand with a creative campaign, but another entirely to be confident that our efforts will hit the right notes with consumers – it might take several attempts to get it right.

Finally, every growth strategy – however well executed – plays out within an environment that is beyond our control. We are therefore always dealing with relative probabilities, not certainties. Besides, any given strategy will have different risks and payoffs associated with it. For example, we might believe that the most effective growth strategy for our business would be to retain more customers, so prioritise keeping the ones we have over acquiring more. Yet if the reasons people stop buying are beyond our control – which they typically are – a loyalty-first strategy might be far riskier than we think.

Consequently, while we can certainly formulate a growth strategy based on solid principles, we must still play a numbers game where experimentation and iteration are key, and where we evaluate our options not just in terms of their potential upsides and downsides, but their *relative growth potential*. With these considerations in mind, let's explore these growth opportunities, starting with the two most basic levers that affect our profits: revenues and costs.

Revenues and costs

In the simplest terms, we can grow our profits either by increasing revenues, decreasing costs, or both. So which should we do?

Obviously it doesn't make sense for any business to be

wasteful, but successful enterprises tend to pursue growth by increasing revenues rather than decreasing costs. Why should that be?[1]

First, companies are typically valued via a multiple of their revenues. It follows, therefore, that revenues hog people's attention, not least because tremendous wealth can be generated through rising valuations, even if the business in question is loss-making or profit margins are slim. Uber, for example, has lost staggering amounts of money, yet former CEO Travis Kalanick was still able to sell his shares for an estimated $2.7 billion with the business never having made a profit.[2]

Second, if top-line revenue grows, it may well be possible to achieve cost reductions through the economies of scale that a larger business offers.

Third, while cost-cutting might increase our profits, efficiency often comes not just at the expense of adaptability – which is crucial if we are to respond to change and explore new opportunities – but of effectiveness in general, especially our ability to create value for customers. It's all too easy to cut back on customer service, quality or advertising, for example, eroding the prominence and appeal of our brand.

Finally, growth also requires fuel, which typically means spending money, not saving it. Just as we need more calories to build muscle than to maintain our current physique, we must have resources to invest if we want to grow – especially at speed. A common mistake among startups, for example, is not raising enough money to allow them to build momentum within their narrow window of opportunity.

Holding a probabilistic model of business firmly in mind, we can therefore postulate our first growth guideline based on what offers the greatest probability of success: *assuming sound financial health, prioritise revenue growth over cost reduction.*

Pricing

When it comes to increasing our revenues, there are two simple variables at play: price and volume. These aren't mutually exclusive – we can optimise our prices *and* try to sell more – but they are nevertheless related. Many products sell in greater volumes when the price is lowered. Others, known as *Veblen goods*, are perceived as exclusive, or high quality, so can actually sell better if the price is increased.

Either way, at anything other than the optimum price, we're leaving profit on the table by undercharging, or sacrificing volume by overcharging. And even small price changes can have a seemingly disproportionate impact on profits, as the following example demonstrates.

Imagine our business sells ceramic frogs as garden ornaments. Each costs $15 to make and we retail them at $20. Each frog sold therefore contributes $5 towards our overheads and profitability. For the sake of simplicity, let's assume the entire $5 is profit. If we now reduce the price of our frog by just a dollar – from $20 to $19 – we've simultaneously reduced our profit margin from $5 to $4. That may not seem much, but by cutting our price by a seemingly cautious five per cent, we've reduced our profit by a whopping twenty per cent.

People who have never given pricing much thought are always staggered when they see this simple set of calculations, and are left attempting to compute how much revenue and profit they might have missed out on by either never considering pricing (let alone experimenting with changes), or by offering discounts without calculating the implications for the bottom line. And yet a casual approach to pricing is surprisingly prevalent. Take the physical therapy clinic I use. They offered me a $50 discount for each hour-long session after my trial visit, before I'd even had the chance to sign up at full price. How many sessions have I attended? Maybe 40. That's $2,000 of profit gone. Let's say they have 200 patients a year who are just like me. Now we're at $400,000. Over the next five years this small business could easily blow $2,000,000 of pure profit just through their discounting policy.

Fortunately there are established techniques for researching and setting prices.[3] In scenarios where requirements are straightforward and there are a large number of alternatives, for example, most customers tend to pick from the middle of the price range – an insight that can help us set our price point.[4] There are also more advanced techniques, such as *conjoint analysis*, that can help establish the relationship between willingness to pay and specific attributes of a product or service. And while a measure of uncertainty is bound to apply, most people are in a position to experiment with price changes – especially if they sell online or through a traditional consultative selling process in a business-to-business environment.

In summary then, since price optimisation gets us a larger contribution margin per sale and may also increase our sales volumes, we arrive at our second guideline: *proactively manage prices to avoid leaving revenues on the table.*

Remember: setting prices is like brushing your teeth. We don't do it just once and forget about it. As our product, brand, awareness and category develop, we must keep revisiting our pricing to make sure we're not needlessly sacrificing revenue.

Acquisition and loyalty

Now that we've tackled pricing, our attention turns to volume. The question is, which is more conducive to increasing sales: attracting new customers or encouraging our existing customers to buy more?

The evidence here is abundantly clear, even if many continue to ignore it: *brands grow primarily through acquiring more customers, not through deepening loyalty*. This point is worth exploring in some detail.

Let's start with an extreme example and imagine we adopt a *loyalty only* strategy. Taking to heart the popular dictum that it costs more to acquire a customer than to keep one, we decide to stick with just *one* customer and devote our attention to them wholeheartedly. What could possibly go wrong?

First, they will come to dominate at the negotiating table. If they want a price discount, better payment terms or the moon on a spoon, we'll have no choice but to give it to them and watch our profits evaporate. Second, if for some reason they stop buying our product, our business will collapse overnight.

Clearly, then, having one big customer is a bad idea, but it's also a common occurrence. Many enterprises, having harpooned a whale-sized client, bend over backwards to keep that client happy to the exclusion of seeking new business. Then one day their big client has a change in leadership, procurement policy, or a spending cut and – POOF! – the business is in dire straits.

I think, for example, of the suppliers who depended on Boeing for the majority of their revenues, and were plunged into crisis by the safety issues around the 737 Max. When Boeing stopped manufacturing – an unanticipated event – and with few other customers in the wings, their businesses faced serious difficulties almost immediately.[5]

In contrast, having many customers not only limits their individual bargaining power, it protects our profits. When we consider the inherent uncertainties of our environment, broadening our customer base also reduces our exposure to risk because if we lose some customers, we still have others. And lose some we will, because – in keeping with the central theme of this book – customers tend to stop buying for reasons beyond our control.

Contrary to popular belief, customers seldom leave as a protest against lacklustre service, although some certainly do. One paper that looked at financial services brands, for example, concluded that only four per cent of customer defection was down to poor service, while a whopping sixty per cent of brand defection was beyond marketers' control.[6]

Instead, what typically causes customers to stop buying is a change in their own circumstances. They may no longer need what we have to offer. They may have taken the decision to move on to a new job or operate somewhere else. They might just feel like changing things up a bit. After all, few people eat at the same restaurant every time they go out, even if they might have a favourite. Yet many executives continue to believe that customer attrition can be massively reduced or even prevented entirely through loyalty schemes, many of which simply compromise the profitability of their highest-spending customers.

Hang on a second, though. What if we *could* substantially reduce the number of customers who leave? Assuming we kept acquisition at current levels, wouldn't that be a sound growth strategy? Isn't it stupid to pour water into a leaky bucket?

Yes – if we're bleeding customers because our product is no longer competitive, we've been embroiled in a scandal, or terrible service is driving them away, these problems warrant urgent attention. In any case, keeping customers satisfied is essential for every business, not least because poor satisfaction will likely affect our ability to acquire new customers. Hundreds of one-star reviews on TripAdvisor, Yelp or TrustPilot aren't exactly a magnet for prospects, and of course we should do what we can to retain our existing customers and increase the amount they spend with us – more on that later.

The more pertinent question is whether retention offers *greater growth potential* than acquisition, relatively speaking, and how much resource we should allocate to each. With the right data, this is something we can work out for ourselves.

Let's say that a quarter of our customers leave every year, and we replace them with new ones through sales and marketing activity. The result, for the sake of argument, is a stable four per cent market share.

If we could somehow retain 100 per cent of our customers – parking for a minute the impossibility of doing so – we'd increase our market share by a maximum of one per cent if our current rate of customer acquisition stays the same. But if a quarter of buyers in the market are switching brands, how much could we theoretically grow our market share if we were to acquire them all?

It's not the measly one per cent the retention strategy offers, it's *twenty-five per cent* – a much bigger opportunity, which if pursued could be like filling the metaphorical leaky bucket with a firehose. Yet the arguments in favour of acquisition don't stop there. Customer loyalty actually *increases*, the more customers we have, on account of a phenomenon known as *the law of double jeopardy*.[7] Let me explain why.

The revenue distribution of established brands does not follow the famous 80/20 rule we're often taught. Instead, just over half of revenues tend to come from the top twenty per cent of customers, and the rest from a large number of light buyers.

These light buyers make infrequent purchases, so tend to buy whichever brand they remember, is readily available, or both – something that favours the biggest brands. Even if you don't drink much coffee, you've probably heard of Starbucks, and there seems to be one on every street corner, making a purchase easy.

This is where the law of double jeopardy gets its name. Smaller brands have fewer customers (the first jeopardy), who are also less loyal on average (the second jeopardy) because light buyers tend to gravitate towards bigger rivals that are more salient and easier to purchase from.

This is why market-leading brands have lots of customers with a long tail of light buyers, rather than comparatively few customers who spend a lot. One exception seemed to be Wells Fargo, whose customers once appeared to have an insatiable appetite for their products that confounded double jeopardy. But there was a simple explanation for that: fraud on an epic scale.[8]

While the law of double jeopardy may clash violently with the near-pervasive belief in a high-engagement, loyalty-first approach to growth, there are now seven decades of supporting evidence gathered from every category and geography imaginable that demonstrates its wisdom. Light buyers are not to be neglected. There are lots of them out there. And there is plenty of room to gain more of their custom. Heavy buyers, by contrast, have probably already reached the limit of what they are prepared to buy.

It's not just that attracting more non-customers and light buyers to our brand offers growth opportunities. It helps with word of mouth, too. Contrary to popular belief, it is not long-standing loyalists who broadcast their enthusiasm, but new customers. Think about it: we are far more likely to discuss a recent purchase or novel experience than something routine, or that's been part of the fabric of our lives for decades.[9] And in consolidating these findings we therefore arrive at another general guideline: *constantly acquire more customers.*

 The fact remains, though, that according to a Gartner study from 2021, seventy-three per cent of chief marketing officers intended to rely on existing customers to fuel growth over the following year.[10] Perhaps a desire to avoid risk explains this strategic misstep. Perhaps simple ignorance. Another likely factor, however, is that people can easily misinterpret their own data. If we are unaware of the principles of double jeopardy, we might assume that low loyalty levels are *the reason for poor market share*, when in fact *they are the result of it*. We might therefore double down on retention – the incorrect strategy.

 On the very rare occurrence that we see a brand with unusually high loyalty given the small size of their customer base, we might also think there is something exceptional or magical about them, rather than that they're keeping a small number of similar customers happy but are terrible at acquiring new ones – a more likely explanation.

 To further muddy the data lake, market share also skews satisfaction scores for a simple reason that seems obvious when we know it: the more customers we have, the broader their spectrum of needs, and the harder it becomes to keep everyone happy.

 That's why many of the world's bestselling books – to take just one example – have lower ratings than we might expect. Once you're selling hundreds of thousands or millions of copies, you're bound to pick up a proportion of readers who can't be satisfied. There are too many wizards in Harry Potter: one star.

The same is true with companies. Small brands with relatively few customers tend to have higher satisfaction scores, and massive brands tend to have poorer ones. In 2018, for example, Volvo topped the leaderboard for customer satisfaction in the US according to J.D. Power, while Ford was near the bottom. Yet Ford outsells Volvo seventeen cars to one.[11]

If you were Ford, you might look at these scores and conclude that you must drastically overhaul the customer experience, not least because the optics of a low rating don't look too good. But Ford's customer care is probably not as bad as the scores suggest – it's just that the company has a lot more customers to keep happy. It's worth bearing in mind that in this context research suggests that pursuing ever-higher satisfaction scores and increasing market share are incompatible goals.[12]

I shudder to think how many ill-informed strategic decisions have been made as a consequence of misinterpreting this kind of data, and thank my lucky stars to have colleagues who really understand this stuff.

Mental availability and buyability

Turning our attention more directly to customer acquisition then, we have another two options to consider. Do we attract more customers by increasing *mental availability* – making our product come to mind more readily in buying situations – or by improving *buyability* – making the products or services themselves easier to buy and more appealing?[13] The answer is both: we want to grow them in parallel, and if we get this right both activities should improve repeat business with existing customers too. Let's take them one at a time, starting with mental availability.

We want our brand to come to mind for as many potential

customers as possible when a need arises, and to be sufficiently distinctive from the competition to stand out – both
of which increase the likelihood of a purchase. As we strive
to achieve these goals, we need to bear in mind that there are
three aspects to building mental availability: *reach*, *relevance*
and *recognition*.[14]

Reach, relevance and recognition

If we want to build our brand's mental availability, the first consideration is who to target those activities towards. Fortunately,
the rule of double jeopardy provides the answer. Knowing
as we do that brands grow primarily through acquiring new
customers, that light buyers constitute the vast majority of
customers, and that it's hard to get heavy buyers to buy more,
reaching non-customers and light buyers is a key objective
because they are a more probable growth opportunity. Furthermore, as we reach out to light buyers, heavy buyers and other
current customers are bound to notice. And since acquisition
usually depends on taking customers from competitors who
satisfy similar needs, a logical approach that offers the greatest
likelihood of success is to target the entire category.

Quorn, which manufactures a meat substitute product,
demonstrates this principle in action. If you were Quorn you'd
be tempted to market your product to vegetarians: the obvious target buyers. However, vegetarians still represent only a
very small percentage of the total population, so such a strategy
promises only limited potential for growth. Recognising this,
Quorn repositioned themselves as a healthy-eating brand. This
has broadened their appeal to a much larger potential range of
buyers – a penetration-based strategy that led to sixty-two per
cent growth by the end of 2011.[15]

Quorn also illustrates another crucial principle when it comes to building mental availability: the desirability of connecting our brand, product or service to the contextual triggers – known as *category entry points* – that prompt buyers to think of relevant brands that might meet their needs. For example, just as Quorn now triggers thoughts of healthy eating, category entry points for a product such as coffee might be waking up, feeling low on energy, getting together with a friend or taking a break. For champagne, they might be a celebration, feeling luxurious, buying a special gift for a friend, or when we're out partying.[16]

A crucial step in building mental availability is therefore to establish the relevance of our brand by attaching it to the category entry points that exist within the buyer's mind through our advertising and communications. This should increase the likelihood of them making a purchase. How, though, do we approach this in practice?

First, bear in mind that when establishing a new brand, the primary objective should not be to educate prospective buyers on what makes us different or special, but simply to attach our brand to a category in the buyer's mind – a basic goal that is often overlooked.

We are told, for example, that startups should try to create a new category if they want to win big. The problem comes when we extend this idea to our communications and promotional activities, because consumers think in a specific way: need, category, brand – *more natural light, window, Velux*, for example.

By implication, unless we attach our brand to a category the buyer already knows and understands, it is less likely to be purchased. Even highly innovative products must be positioned in familiar terms to make them buyable. Tesla, for example, initially marketed their products not as semi-autonomous electric vehicles but as cars with zero emissions. The company knew that *cars* and *emissions* were already familiar concepts in buyers' minds.

The second thing we should appreciate is that not all category entry points are equally important. We should therefore focus on the most relevant and common ones – the ones that stand the highest chance of leading to a purchase. Attaching Coca-Cola to such category entry points as *quench thirst, hot day*, or *family get-together* makes sense. Attaching it to *blood stains* – which it reportedly removes very well – or *making Kalimotxo*, a Spanish drink in which cola and red wine are mixed in equal measure (and which sounds pretty horrendous to me), is not a wise step.

Finally, since our aim is to achieve a sale, making our brand relevant in a broader range of buying scenarios by attaching it to more category entry points should be a key part of our strategy, rather than focusing all our attention on trying to own one or two. Here, then, is another growth guideline that can increase our odds of success: *communicate your relevance to as many potential buyers as possible.*

These strategies will be compromised, however, if our products are not also easy to recognise. At my local supermarket, for example, there is a shelf that runs from the checkouts at the front to the meat counter at the back – about eighty feet – stocked solely with brands of granola. I'm sure they're all very tasty, but how on earth am I supposed to choose one? If it's frustrating to me, it must be equally frustrating to the manufacturers. They manage to secure distribution of their brand with a major grocery chain, only to find that their products are hiding in plain sight among all the other brands.

To avoid this common problem and increase the likelihood

of a sale, we must cultivate and consistently use distinctive brand assets that make our products more noticeable and easier to find.[17] The silhouette of a Porsche 911 or the shape of the Coca-Cola bottle are great examples of distinctive assets. So too are T-Mobile's eye-popping magenta and McDonald's golden arches – neither of which has anything to do with mobile phones or fast food, just as George Clooney has no inherent associations with coffee or tequila. Distinctive assets can be totally meaningless in isolation, yet work perfectly well regardless.

We can also extend this distinctiveness beyond the visual. Just as we may cultivate our own distinctive tone of voice or way with words, there is no reason at all why we can't form a distinctive in-store experience or *experiential signature* more broadly. Either will help make our brand more memorable.

What we definitely don't want to do is blend in with our rivals by using the same style, tone or colour palette, or worse still, replace existing distinctive assets for the sake of novelty, since this will impair recognition and reduce the likelihood of a purchase, as certain high-profile examples demonstrate.

Tropicana's decision to change their long-established, instantly recognisable packaging for something generic and bland confused consumers and was swiftly reversed – a $50 million exercise that caused sales to drop twenty per cent within two months.[18] Similarly, in 2010 Gap Inc. replaced their iconic logo with something that looked like a hasty Power-Point mockup, only to go back to the old one seven days later – another colossal waste of money.[19] Lesson learned, we now have another growth guideline: *cultivate distinctive assets that make your brand easier to recognise and recall.*

Yet it doesn't matter how much awareness we generate if our products and services cannot be bought. Ideally, we want our offerings to be available where and when it suits the customer, to be easy to choose and purchase, and suitable for a broad range of buying situations or needs – all of which can increase the probability of a purchase. Let's explore these options in more detail.

Channel and territory selection

If we want to make our products or services easy to buy for as many people as possible, our first step is to sell through the channels that our customers find most convenient and use habitually.[20]

Many brands, for example, are available to purchase through major e-commerce and physical retailers as well as their own websites and stores, over the phone or at kiosks. By making their offerings available through as many popular channels as possible, the enterprises behind them increase the likelihood of a purchase.

They don't typically start out this way, however. Many products are initially sold door-to-door, from the boot of a car or to friends. When word starts to spread, the business might launch a small shop or e-commerce offering, then expand their footprint from there.

Another option is to cover not just more channels but more territories, too. An obvious path to growth for many businesses is simply to start selling across a broader range of geographies where there are more customers to serve – assuming we can build awareness in those territories. This gives us another guideline: *maximise the availability of your offerings by covering more channels and territories.*

It's not just making the product physically available that matters, though, we also want to make our products as easy to choose and purchase as possible – regardless of the channel or territory. We do this by lowering the barriers to purchase. Let's look at those barriers now.

Lowering barriers to purchase

Purchasing barriers fall into three categories:

1. **Operational barriers:** installation headaches, compatibility problems and limited distribution, for example.
2. **Experiential barriers:** trialability, choice paralysis, onerous transactions, the need for training and expertise, or clashes with existing learned behaviours.
3. **Financial barriers:** the upfront purchase price, or the switching costs to get started with a new offering.[21]

Any one of these barriers can be the difference between success or failure, or can transform our ability to acquire new customers. So it makes sense to identify any and every potential barrier and then get to work on lowering them.

We might allow people to spread the cost of our product over multiple payments to make the price point more accessible. If we're a software company, we might want to ensure that it's easy to import data from rival systems into our own, which lowers potential customers' switching costs. We could also find ways for customers to trial our product or service so that they can experience the benefits more quickly, and with no financial risk, or make choosing and purchasing the right product less onerous.

The subscription wine-club business Winc is a great example. Rather than assume that customers are experts on different grapes, regions or brands, and ask them to peruse thousands of bottles to pick the ones they like, Winc customers take a profiling quiz, answering questions about how they take their coffee, whether they put much salt on their food, and so on, then the website recommends the bottles that the customer is most likely to enjoy. The business has flourished since launching in 2012.

Almost regardless of our line of business, our customers will face similar challenges to that of the prospective wine purchaser. We therefore arrive at another growth guideline that can increase our odds of success: *systematically dismantle purchasing and adoption barriers to maximise conversion.*

Extending the range

Another way to enhance the buyability of our products or services is to cover a broader range of buying scenarios. One option might be to adopt a simple versioning strategy that allows people to buy in different sizes or at different quality or feature levels. Another is to increase share of wallet – management jargon for the amount customers spend with us as opposed to our rivals – by satisfying the unmet needs that our customers currently turn to competitors for.

Let's say I divide my grocery shopping between two brands. Brand A has smaller, nicer stores, wonderful customer service, a small range of high-quality produce, and premium prices. Brand B has huge yet comparatively unappealing stores and offers humdrum service, but sells a much larger range of goods at lower prices. I shop at Brand A for fresh fruit, vegetables, meat and fish. For boring domestic necessities, I turn to Brand B.

Brand A can improve the quality of their food, customer

service or store ambiance all they like – they may consider these to be the *satisfaction drivers* that affect customer perceptions of their business. But doing so won't make me spend any more with them; I shop with Brand B because they meet different needs. Conversely, Brand B can lower their prices all they like, but it won't make me spend any less with Brand A.

While improving what they already do might lead to higher satisfaction scores, the bigger opportunities – the *growth drivers* – for each brand are the unmet needs that cause customers to spend elsewhere.[22]

Brand A, for example, could introduce a lower-priced range, which is exactly what premium supermarkets have done on both sides of the Atlantic. Waitrose in the UK introduced an *Essentials* range, which happens to include flageolet beans, Ardennes pâté, Cypriot halloumi and helicopter fuel – essentials indeed – and Whole Foods in the US introduced 365, a similar value range aimed at more price-conscious buyers.[23]

It may even be sufficient to neutralise, rather than outperform, the rival's natural advantage. Waitrose and Whole Foods' value ranges might get away with being a little more expensive than their rivals, but still be cheap enough that customers can rationalise the higher-quality purchase.[24]

Unfortunately, many brands mistakenly assume that satisfaction and growth drivers must be the same thing, and so focus on doing what they already do better than rival brands, rather than giving customers reasons to stop using alternatives – which is a more alluring avenue to growth.

We can therefore grow not only by versioning our product to cater to a broader range of price points, but also to a broader range of needs. In other words, we can *expand the range to cover a broader spectrum of buying scenarios and needs.*

Continuous improvement

While we're pursuing all these opportunities, though, we mustn't forget that business success is predicated on creating value for customers, and that the greater their perception of value, the more successful we're likely to be. But where does that value come from? There are four underlying sources.

First and foremost, the *product or service* itself – what it does and what it costs.

Then there's the appeal of the *brand* – the extent to which it is associated with particular qualities, categories, or expectations.

Awareness is also vital – people can't value something they don't know exists, and they tend to find familiar brands, products or services more appealing and easier to recall when a buying need arises.

Finally, there's *customer experience* – the continuum of interactions that customers have with us – which can add additional value beyond the product in the form of, for example, exceptional customer service, onboarding, purchasing experiences or after-sales support.

We've already touched on all of these aspects of value creation in one way or another, highlighting the importance of building mental availability, for example, and the benefits that versioning the product has to offer.

The reality, however, is that expectations tend to rise over time. And certainly, during the early years of our brand, product or category there will be ample room for improvement across all of these areas – not least in the performance of the product or service itself. As I look at the objects on my desk, for example, I see an external hard drive whose capacity was unimaginable two decades ago, a smartphone whose processing power, battery life, camera and operating system are in another league from the first version, and a laptop that is lighter, faster and has a higher-resolution screen than its predecessor.

I think too about just how much has changed around how these products are purchased. I recently ordered a pair of headphones online that arrived at my doorstep within two hours – an impressive logistical feat. Soon, I suspect, such service will be normalised.

As entrepreneur Jim Jannard once remarked, 'Everything in the world can and will be made better . . . the only questions are, "when and by whom?"'[25] Our answer should be *now, and by us*. Remember – we do not need to predict the future if we're out in front creating it.

Yes, it is possible to overshoot – making products that are too good for our customers' needs. Yet it's also easy to lose sight of the fact that we are in a race against rising expectations that force us to continually improve our products, services and the customer experience more broadly. And in our noisy, cluttered world, we must continually invest in our brand and awareness to avoid being forgotten.

Resting on our laurels is a recipe for disaster, then, so we have another growth guideline to consider: *increase the customer's perception of value through continuous improvement*.

To make the most of our value creation efforts, I would recommend an integrated approach, where we treat sources of value as intrinsically linked. We gain more from our awareness, brand-building and customer experience efforts if the expectations set through our communications are met in reality. Similarly, we create more value for customers if our products and services are seamlessly integrated into the broader experience of being a customer. And we can further strengthen our brand if we create a customer experience that is consciously distinctive. If we can do these things – and make sure our improvements are actually noticeable – we will take care of customer retention by proxy.

The clothing company Patagonia offers a great example. They actively demonstrate their environmentally-friendly values through their activism, donations to grassroots organisations, services (such as free repairs on their items) and product development efforts – all of which focus on reducing their environmental impact. Their customer service is consistently excellent, and their products are both well designed and well made. Every aspect of value creation works to amplify the others, which goes a long way to explaining why I'm wearing a Patagonia fleece, trousers and underpants as I write this.

Exploitation and exploration

Thus far, all the paths to growth we've considered fall under the banner of *exploitation*: ways to grow existing product lines, services or business units that have already achieved product-market fit.

Eventually, however, every party must come to an end. Advantages will be competed away. Categories will saturate, or decline and become less profitable. Exploitation, unfortunately, has limited potential.

Yet it is not our only option. We also have *exploration*: creating entirely new products or services, perhaps even in different categories. And to fulfil our growth potential we must use both approaches: exploiting existing opportunities as well as exploring entirely new ones.

Why? The reasons for exploitation are obvious enough. There's no point leaving money on the table after the hard work and risks involved with getting a new venture off the ground. And in competitive markets, to stand still is to go backwards.

But exploration is also essential if we are to sow the seeds of opportunity for the future. The potential payoffs can be far larger too, since we can create additional ventures that can also grow through exploitation if they take off.

As Jeff Bezos explained in a letter to shareholders: 'Sometimes (often actually) in business, you *do* know where you're going, and when you do, you can be efficient. Put in place a plan and execute.

In contrast,' he continues, 'wandering in business is not efficient . . . but it's also not random. It's [. . .] powered by a deep conviction that the prize for customers is big enough that it's worth being a little messy and tangential to find our way there. Wandering is an essential counter-balance to efficiency. You need to employ both. The outsized discoveries – the "non-linear" ones – are highly likely to require wandering.'[26]

In appreciating this cycle of exploration and exploitation we can now resolve a paradox that few within marketing and product development seem able to get their heads around: celebrated entrepreneurs are often known to be profoundly customer-focused, while simultaneously showing little regard for traditional market research.

The reason is simple: most market research techniques are geared towards *exploitation*, which offers mostly linear payoffs by helping brands innovate *in response* to the customer. These methods are valuable within that context, but don't help as much in an uncertain world where we must explore, place bets, nurture the ideas that show promise and kill the rest. To achieve those goals we need to be comfortable with uncertainty, willing to take risks and innovate *on behalf* of the customer. There is no data from the future.

This also explains, at least in part, why so few large corporations manage to enter and dominate future growth markets away from their core lines of business, and often miss massive opportunities altogether. It stems from a pathological rejection of uncertainty.

The larger the company, the larger the opportunities it must pursue to meet ambitious growth targets. If it turns over a million dollars a year, it can grow ten per cent by adding a hundred thousand dollars in revenue. If it generates $10 billion a year, it needs to find an extra billion to achieve the same growth rate – a big ask given that most mature markets are both relatively static and intensely competitive.

Faced with a situation where vast sums of money need to roll in to satisfy shareholders and industry analysts, focusing on exploitation seems easier and less risky than exploration. Entering what may superficially appear to be a tiny market that is riddled with unknown risks and unclear upsides – even if it's growing fast – is less appealing. It can't sate our company's whale-sized appetite today, and what it might offer in the future is far from certain. Consequently, the idea of exploration – placing a handful of small bets where most may fail but a single winner could achieve phenomenal results – is often anathema to risk-averse senior managers. They consider it irresponsible to greenlight a project that might fail.

Yet although exploitation seems efficient, effective, logical and more predictable, it is not enough. An exclusive focus on incremental improvements to existing products or services is risky in the long run. And if we wait until a new market is large and stable enough to be of interest, we'll find that it now belongs to other brands that tinkered, experimented and learned what works along the way.[27]

What, then, should we do?

Staying true to the entrepreneurial methods outlined in the previous chapter, we need to work from the basis of affordable loss and begin to place bets on promising new ideas. While some of our ideas might not take off, we need only one big hit for the payoff to more than compensate for our failures.

When IAC was the parent company of Match.com, they took an exploratory approach to growth by funding their own startup incubator Hatch Labs with $6 million.[28] They had only one success, but that success happened to be the dating app Tinder, which is now worth billions of dollars in its own right.[29] Incremental improvements to Match.com would never have achieved the same outcome.

Another inspiring example is Ustwo, a digital design studio whose bread-and-butter work is designing websites and apps for clients. This is a time and materials business, so growth through exploitation is a relatively linear path to tread – adding more staff or offices to serve more clients. However, Ustwo has also taken an exploratory approach to development, combining their exceptional talents and creativity to make a computer game, *Monument Valley*, which has grossed $25 million in four years – a 17x return on the $1.4 million Ustwo spent on development. It's the kind of jumbo payoff that would have been impossible had they simply focused on developing their agency business.[30] *Monument Valley* has also produced a synergistic benefit, raising awareness of Ustwo's brand and so attracting more clients to their core design business.

The final growth guideline, then, is this: *combine exploitation of existing opportunities with exploration of new categories and offerings to maximise your growth potential.*

The ten paths to growth

1. Assuming sound financial health, prioritise revenue growth over cost reduction.
2. Proactively manage prices to avoid leaving revenues on the table.
3. Constantly acquire more customers.
4. Communicate your relevance to as many potential buyers as possible.
5. Cultivate distinctive assets that make your brand easier to recognise and recall.
6. Maximise the availability of your offerings by covering more channels and territories.
7. Systematically dismantle purchasing and adoption barriers.
8. Expand the range to cover a broader spectrum of buying scenarios and needs.
9. Increase the customer's perception of value through continuous improvement.
10. Combine exploitation with exploration to maximise your growth potential.

How, though, do we apply these guidelines in practice? There are two approaches we can employ: an alluringly simple top-down approach, and a slightly messier project-based approach.

Defining your growth strategy

The top-down approach is to discover the points of maximum leverage – the growth opportunities that are most likely to offer the biggest potential returns – and elevate them to commercial priorities.

Some businesses have never considered pricing, for example, which is an obvious place to start. Others do not devote enough effort to acquiring new customers. Yet more generate plenty of awareness but experience horrendous conversion rates and customer acquisition costs because of barriers that make purchasing difficult. Some are so focused on satisfaction drivers that they ignore unmet needs. Others experience a much more fundamental problem: products and services that simply aren't competitive.

As a consequence, we should evaluate our operation with a critical eye and pursue the growth opportunities that best suit our context. The near-miraculous turnaround of Domino's Pizza, whose share price rose 1,300 per cent under CEO J. Patrick Doyle, is a tremendous example.[31]

At their lowest ebb, Domino's most obvious problem was the pizza itself, which tasted ghastly. They therefore set about improving the recipes until their pizzas tasted better than those of their biggest rivals. Then they began transforming the basic customer experience, introducing, for example, the now-famous pizza tracker that allows customers to see the progress of their order. At a stroke they enhanced customer perceptions of value where it mattered most: taste and convenience.

While these improvements were underway, Domino's launched a highly creative brand campaign that got people's attention by admitting how badly they'd messed things up and what they were doing about it.

Next, Domino's began investing heavily in technology to make purchasing as effortless as possible. You can now order Domino's through a bewildering array of channels beyond their physical stores, website or app, including Alexa, Slack and the dashboard of certain Ford cars.[32] Over sixty per cent of their sales now come from digital channels, rather than from traditional pizza-ordering methods such as via the phone or over the counter.[33]

Domino's adopted a top-down approach – and it worked. But this is not always the case.

Even if the leadership can concoct a compelling strategy, success relies on everyone in the business getting it and working from the same assumptions, and that's not something that always – or even usually – happens. In reality, as workshops and client engagements have demonstrated over the years, by the time you trip down the hierarchy a couple of rungs, few have any clear sense of what the company's strategy is. You might also be stepping into a political quagmire, with each department or fiefdom scrapping with the others.

This problem is a natural consequence of the divisional structures and specialisms we find in large organisations – the perfect environment for human tribalism to take root. It's also a problem that is compounded by the fact that each department has an allotted budget to spend. The social media team spends their money on social media initiatives, the customer service team spends their money on customer service improvements, and the marketing communications team spends their money on advertising – that's what the money's for.

The challenge therefore becomes slightly different – how do we make sure our departmental activities help our business grow as a whole?

The key is to see our skills and resources as a means to an end, and to align them to the most promising growth opportunities based on our own clear-headed and broad-ranging analysis of the company's context. Furthermore, we should evaluate the merit of *all* our projects and ideas in service of these opportunities.

It is common, for example, for customer experience professionals to assume they can add the most value to their organisations through a focus on retention and loyalty, and initiatives that aim to delight heavy buyers – a dangerous conviction that goes some way to explaining the poor returns that many of these programmes deliver.

An analysis of the customer base, their buying behaviour and the competitive context might reveal something else entirely: that their initiatives should instead focus on smoothing the path to purchase for new customers, and improving the overall experience for light buyers where share of wallet could more easily be increased. They might also recognise the value of primary research in understanding which unmet needs are sending customers to rivals. From here, they could also set out to address the most pressing causes of dissatisfaction among the existing buyer base – a defensive measure against defection as well as a growth strategy. Of course they could conclude something else entirely – that the biggest challenge facing the business is poor awareness, in which case they might set out to create some truly remarkable or memorable interactions that generate buzz among potential buyers.

Either way, once these opportunities have been identified, a robust proposal can be assembled, management can be lobbied for funding, and experiments can be run to test hypotheses.

All of which relies, of course, on a willingness within the company to see beyond departmental lines, broaden decision-makers' general business knowledge, run experiments, and base decisions on the evidence – a neat segue to the final chapter, which addresses how leadership, people management and culture set us up to fail or succeed in our uncertain world.

Chapter summary

- While no business should aspire to be wasteful, successful enterprises tend to pursue growth through increasing revenues rather than cost reductions.

- Pricing changes have a disproportionate impact on our profit margins. Proactively managing prices is essential to avoid leaving revenues on the table.
- Brands grow primarily by acquiring more customers, not by deepening loyalty.
- We can attract more customers through improving mental availability and buyability.
- To raise awareness we should focus on reach, relevance and recognition.
- We can improve buyability by covering more sales channels and territories.
- Ensuring our brand, products and services are distinctive makes them easier to recognise.
- Reducing operational, experiential and financial barriers to purchase can increase sales.
- Another option is to expand the range to cover a broader spectrum of buying scenarios, catering to unmet needs that drive customers to competitors.
- We must aim to increase the customer's perception of value through continuous improvement across four areas: improving the product or service itself, strengthening the appeal of the brand, raising awareness and improving the customer experience.
- To fulfil our growth potential we must combine *exploitation* – growing existing product lines, services or business units, and *exploration* – creating entirely new opportunities.
- The ideal approach to growth is to discover the points of maximum leverage – the growth opportunities that will offer the biggest potential returns – and focus on them.
- Departmental initiatives should be conceived and evaluated in light of the most opportune growth areas.

8 Lessons for leaders
Managing in an unpredictable world

Pet peeves. Everyone I know has them, and I'm certainly no exception. One of mine, which seems to feature in every panel discussion or conference at some point, is earnest monologues that begin: '*We need to change the culture.*'

'We need to change the culture of banking' is one I've heard a few times. No luck so far, incidentally. And new CEOs who are tasked with stamping out scandalous behaviour in any business usually make *changing the culture* a featured phrase in their apology tour to customers, regulators and employees – changes that I'm sure would be beneficial for all. So why does the expression irritate me so much?

Part of my ire arises from the yawning chasm between the triteness of the remark and the reality of what's involved. What's on my to-do list for today ... let me see. Buy some eggs, pick up the dry cleaning, change the culture of a global, multitrillion-dollar industry. And there is also an element of pedantry, which I make no apology for. When people say 'We need to change the culture', the relationship of verb and object in the sentence implies that culture is in fact something that can just be changed, like the tyres on a car.

But culture is not like that. It defies such direct manipulation – you can't just lift and shift it. Furthermore, this innocuous-sounding remark defies the purpose of culture itself – to bring stability and cohesion to a social group by reinforcing normative behaviours, and buffering the forces that alter them. The central feature of culture is that it *resists* change.

This is not to say that culture is set in stone, though. It can and does evolve, often through deliberate action to effect a change in people's behaviour. And culture's other soft siblings – leadership and management in particular – are vital considerations too. Applying the lessons in this book at any level beyond the individual requires certain organisational characteristics which have direct implications for how people are hired, managed and incentivised.

It's one thing to say, for example, that we must be willing to fail. But if our leaders disagree, we've got a problem. Similarly, it's all very well for us to recommend drawing on a plurality of perspectives to arrive at better decisions, but how possible is that if all the decision-makers within an organisation are the same age, gender, nationality, social class and ethnic group, and have the same education?

With these thoughts in mind, this final chapter explores the organisational traits we need to thrive under conditions of uncertainty. Beginning, somewhat ironically, with questioning the value of goals themselves.

Destructive goal pursuit

A couple of years ago a friend announced that he'd begun training for a gruelling ultra-marathon later in the year: fifty kilometres through savage terrain in the roasting Californian summer.

Party pooper that I am, I tried to talk him out of it. I'm a keen runner myself, with first-hand experience of what happens when you switch overnight from a sedentary existence to heavy training. Unless you put solid foundations in place first – good mobility, flexibility and core strength – injury is a foregone conclusion.

He threw himself into the challenge anyway, and began racking up the miles. Soon he was grumbling about knee pain, but he stuck to the programme. A few months later he entered a marathon as a training event, even though he was in agony – it was on his plan, after all – and spent the following two weeks on crutches. He never set foot on the start line of the big event and has been unable to run at all since. Rather than abandon or modify his goal in response to emerging conditions, he kept at it and suffered the consequences.

This *destructive goal pursuit* is a surprisingly common phenomenon, and in extreme cases it can be fatal. Every year, for example, people die on Mount Everest from *summit fever*. They become so focused on reaching the top that they persevere in the face of lethal weather conditions and never make it back down.

Might we face similar risks in a business context? It's not something many consider because they are so preoccupied with the *benefits* of goal-setting. Goals provide a North Star to navigate by. They galvanise the workforce in pursuit of a shared objective. And on a personal level, goals are what push us to function and engage with the world around us. They bring a vital sense of meaning to our actions.

There is, however, a growing body of evidence that suggests that rigidly pursuing narrowly defined goals – especially the ambitious kind that management gurus froth about – can be downright dangerous since they are fundamentally at odds with the reality of our complex, unpredictable world.

What if we set an ambitious goal and, as we pursue it, experience a major change in our environment that renders that goal unattainable? Should we pursue it regardless? What if our big hairy audacious goal comes into conflict with other important goals?[1] Should we stick with it, even if the overall consequences for the business might be disastrous?

While the obvious answer to these questions is a resounding 'No!', organisations can become so fixated on what they've set out to do that they ignore to their detriment the inevitable changes in their environment.

General Motors became so committed to winning twenty-nine per cent market share – a somewhat arbitrary figure that they had recently slipped beneath – that they compromised their long-term prospects in the process.[2] Wells Fargo were so determined that each customer should have eight of their products that when they didn't want them, staff created millions of fraudulent accounts to meet their targets.[3] More generally, senior executives freely admit to sacrificing the future of their business to meet short-term analyst expectations – the goal they are often most incentivised to pursue.[4]

Perhaps the single most destructive tendency I've observed in my own career is teams pushing products onto the market to meet a deadline, even when those products are fatally flawed, mistimed, or have no hope of commercial success. BlackBerry, for example, were so desperate to launch an iPad rival that they rushed to market the PlayBook, even though this didn't include native versions of BlackBerry's most important features: their email, contact and calendaring systems. It was a decision that eventually led to a product few wanted, and a $485 million write-down on unsold inventory.[5]

In reality, the process of setting and pursuing appropriate goals is strewn with obstacles and dangers. The goals we set may be the wrong ones; they can be difficult to abandon (even when their continued pursuit is obviously ill-advised); they can encourage foolhardy risk-taking and unethical behaviour; and when the environment is uncertain, their pursuit can make us less effective – if we try to look too far ahead, we can blind ourselves to complex challenges or opportunities in the here and now.[6] Finally, visualising what we believe to be our inevitable victory – a popular technique put forth from the pulpit by motivational speakers – actually hoodwinks the brain into thinking we've already achieved it, which can cause us to strive less, not more.[7]

So what should we do differently?

The key thing is to recognise the conditions that lead to destructive goal pursuit so that we can avoid them. According to Dr Christopher Kayes, an authority on the topic, these conditions include a singular, fixed goal (achieving twenty-nine per cent market share, for example); ambitious goals we've publicly promised will be achieved (for instance, results promised to industry analysts); and goals that become too strongly linked to an individual or group's sense of identity (like those whose mission in life is to conquer Everest).

Kayes also warns against setting goals that reflect an idealised vision of the future and so distract from the complexities of the present. He points to the dangers of aims that are self-justifying, rather than tethered to any other logical grounds for action (for example, pursuing ever-higher quality standards because of an unquenchable lust for perfection). And he counsels against encouraging people to believe that fulfilling a particular goal is a team or individual's destiny. In all such cases, he argues, should unforeseen events then occur, or complexities emerge that require the management of multiple conflicting goals, or a change in situation renders the desired outcome unattainable, continued pursuit of the goal will lead to disaster.

Rather than fall into any of these traps, we should instead set more carefully thought-out, appropriate goals in the first place, and then structure their pursuit in ways that diminish the likelihood of destructive behaviour. In short, we need to be thoughtful and wary. As the authors of the influential paper *Goals Gone Wild* remark, 'Rather than dispensing goal setting as a benign, over-the-counter treatment for motivation, managers and scholars need to conceptualise goal setting as a prescription-strength medication that requires careful dosing, consideration of harmful side effects, and close supervision.'[8]

Often it helps to adopt an entrepreneur's mindset here. When it comes to uncertain environments, for example, it is better to focus on *learning goals* – acquiring certain knowledge, skills or generating ideas – rather than *performance goals*, such as hitting predefined targets.[9] Expert entrepreneurs typically don't start out with revenue or sales targets, or commit to an inflexible vision of the future. They focus on getting feedback from the market as early and cheaply as possible, and assembling a high-performance team that can solve unexpected, complex problems in short order.

Another useful entrepreneurial trick is to avoid using numerical scores and singular metrics as the basis for rewards and recognition. All too often this leads to pathological *metric fixation* – a catalysing agent for destructive goal pursuit, and a topic worth exploring in its own right.

The dangers of metric fixation

As Chapter 2 revealed, today's management orthodoxy is directly descended from Taylor's paradigm of scientific management from over a century ago. So it's unsurprising that business decision-makers today show an irrepressible zeal for measuring everything. If anything, this zeal has increased in recent years, as data-gathering technologies have become ever more powerful.

But while accurate data combined with expert judgement leads to superior decision-making in many, if not most circumstances in business, trouble inevitably sets in if we assume that if we can't measure something it's not worth managing, or only manage what we can easily measure.

The risks of this approach are all too apparent when one considers what happens when the evaluation of individual performance is reduced to what can be measured. It's tempting, for example, to remunerate a salesperson solely on their ability to generate immediate revenue. However, in doing so there is a risk that our salesperson will show little concern for whether the sales they're making are actually profitable or their customer is satisfied. They may also succumb to the temptation to game their numbers to fit in with what has been dictated from on high.

This law of unintended consequences is not just a problem for salespeople. When surgeons are evaluated according to their success rates, they stop operating on difficult cases that might cause their scores to suffer.[10] When police officers are incentivised to reduce the incidence of certain crimes, they reclassify the crimes they solve accordingly – downgrading attempted burglary to trespassing, for example.[11] And when customer service representatives are evaluated on survey scores, they start asking customers to rate them highly. Hence we have Goodhart's Law – that any measure used for control ceases to be a good measure. A common response to Goodhart's Law is usually to add more metrics – an exercise that demands more data, requires more complex systems and processes, and generally means people spend more time reporting their performance than actually performing.

A close friend who works for a global brand shared with me their own experience of the law of unintended consequences. They work in a local market and have to provide regular sales forecasts to the head office, which is overwhelmingly concerned with the accuracy of the forecasts (but apparently not their trajectory), and has historically made its displeasure known if these projections turn out to be incorrect. How has the local market team responded? First, it has reclassified *confirmed* future orders as *forecasted* orders so its predictive data can always be seen to be correct. Second, when an unexpected order comes in it is delayed until it can be 'forecasted'.

The local office's forecasts may be superficially accurate, but they completely misrepresent reality, impede astute decision-making, and the kludge required to generate them undermines the company's ability to actually make money and manage cash flow – the perfect example of how metric fixation and destructive goal pursuit go hand in hand. In the process, securing customer satisfaction and revenue have become secondary considerations.

Measurement can also damage innovation. As Jerry Muller explains in *The Tyranny of Metrics*, 'When people are judged by performance metrics, they are incentivised to do what the metrics measure, and what the metrics measure will be some established goal. But that impedes innovation, which means doing something that is not yet established, indeed hasn't been tried out. Innovation involves experimentation. Trying out something new entails risk, including the possibility, perhaps probability of failure.'[12]

I would go further and argue that the very fact that entrepreneurship entails unknowable elements of risk that simply cannot be measured means that its successful pursuit is incompatible with a culture of metric fixation. Organisations with a culture of obsessive quantification tend to favour projects that yield easy-to-measure incremental improvements in the short term, and shy away from taking risks on ideas that could deliver spectacular returns, but whose return on investment is unknowable in advance. The net result can be a systematic failure to nurture new opportunities that could provide the foundation for even greater growth in the future.

By contrast, successful entrepreneurs embrace the very different notion of affordable loss (see page 154). In so doing – acknowledging that a project may not succeed, let alone have precise payoffs that can be calculated in advance – the team escapes the trap of metric fixation and is liberated to pursue bigger ideas, while keeping the guardrails that allow the organisation to microdose risk in a controllable manner.

What else can we do to retain the fundamental benefits of measuring performance, while limiting the potential downsides?

First and foremost we must recognise that, as Muller concludes, measurement is not an alternative to good judgement, merely an ingredient. We must cultivate not only the expertise to interpret metrics correctly but also the wisdom to know what is worth measuring, how it should be measured, and what incentives those measures might create.

In practical terms this means involving those whose performance will be measured in the process itself – seeking their input on what should be measured, how, and to what standard – and treading a fine line between too few measures (which distorts behaviour) and too many (which is costly and complex to manage). It also means respecting that not everything that can be measured matters, and not everything that matters can be measured. Innovation and creativity, entrepreneurship and exploratory growth are inherently incompatible with a culture of metric fixation. They are also extremely difficult to pursue if the organisation in question has a *negative error culture*.

Negative and positive error cultures

A number of years ago I was asked to critique a new proposition for a large technology company. My findings suggested that the product was unlikely to succeed in its current guise, and I recommended some changes to increase the odds of a favourable outcome.

On reading the report my client said something that is etched into my memory: 'The first thing we need to do is make sure nobody sees this report.' Rather than being shared and debated, the findings were actively suppressed. The project went on to be a disaster. Eventually the division bled so much red ink it was shut down.

My client's attitude is not unusual. If anything, it's the norm within large organisations, where failures and mistakes are not treated as the unavoidable consequences of attempting to learn or grow within a dynamic and unpredictable environment, but as indictments of our competence or character. In such environments, our decision-making becomes *defensive* – driven by avoiding negative outcomes, blame or looking stupid, and while success has many parents, failure has none.

This creates what risk expert Gerd Gigerenzer calls a *negative error culture*. Mistakes are hidden or downplayed, starving decision-makers of the information they need, and making it more difficult to put measures in place to prevent a repeat performance. The costs can be disastrous.[13]

When one compares the safety record of aviation – which has a positive error culture – and medicine – which in the most general terms has a negative error culture – we see the consequences writ large. Air travel is becoming safer and safer, while the World Health Organization reports that one in ten patients is harmed during hospital visits.[14]

The use of basic checklists, for example – a routine part of aviation – is comparatively rare in medicine and the consequences are often tragic. Two-thirds of the 29,000 deaths each year from catheter infections in the US could be prevented by using a basic hygiene checklist, yet even with ten years of data to support their usage, few hospitals have adopted such a practice.[15]

Such a negative error culture won't get us far in an unpredictable world. Instead, we must aspire towards the exact opposite – a *positive error culture* – where fear is replaced by transparency, uncovering and addressing errors is rewarded, teams are encouraged to tinker, experiment and seize the initiative, and lessons are widely shared. How can we seek to realise this goal?

Leaders must set the right example and be willing to report and acknowledge their own errors. Managers must be able to separate the people from the problem when mistakes do occur, then focus their attention on the latent conditions, systems and processes that led to the mistake.

Arguably, nobody has been a greater proponent of creating such a positive error culture in business than investor Ray Dalio, whose Bridgewater hedge fund is the largest in the world. His book *Principles* implores leaders to 'Create a culture in which it is ok to make mistakes and unacceptable not to learn from them.'

Punishing mistakes is counter-productive, he explains. It

leads people to hide their errors, while starving the organisation of valuable information and learning opportunities. Instead, his firm penalises those who conceal or fail to own up to their mistakes, and captures errors in a company-wide report so they can be analysed for patterns and addressed systematically – a standard practice in the safety management industry. Dalio also encourages radical transparency within his organisation to enable accurate information to flow freely.[16]

Another technique we use in our own businesses is running not just project post-mortems, but *pre-mortems*. Starting an engagement, product development process or even the launch of a new venture by proactively acknowledging the risks and possibilities for error sets the correct tone from the outset – one where people are open about their concerns, share the mistakes they've seen in the past and the risks they perceive in the programme.

On some projects, for example – particularly those involving pharmaceutical or financial services companies – we know from past experience that legal or regulatory reviews can delay projects or impose heavy constraints, so we discuss how this can be factored in from day one. On others we've learned that gathering and creating content – copy and images for a website, for example – typically takes far longer than people estimate, and so can hold things up if we don't start that workstream early enough. Yet the potential to have such dialogues in the first place is contingent on the dynamics of the team itself, which brings us onto the vital topic of *psychological safety*.

The need for psychological safety

Why are some teams capable of extraordinary performance and others achieve so much less? That is the question Google sought to answer with Project Aristotle – a near-exhaustive analysis of team effectiveness across hundreds of their work groups.

The most important condition, they concluded, is *psychological safety*: the degree to which members of a team feel safe taking risks and being vulnerable with one another, without the prospect of shame, ridicule or punishment.[17]

This finding should come as no surprise. Our ability to thrive and grow in an uncertain world depends on our ability to innovate and experiment, which in turn depends on our willingness to share ideas in the first place, and accept the possibility that they may not always succeed.

If we are discouraged from sharing ideas through fear of ridicule, and if we're punished or maligned for making mistakes or taking a risk that doesn't work out, we won't bother. Our ability to adapt and grow is also entirely dependent on our ability to learn, which tends to involve asking questions. If people cannot safely question the way things are done, the business stagnates.

As leadership coach and author Timothy Clark explains, the primary task of a leader is therefore to increase *intellectual friction* – the eagerness to embrace a multitude of perspectives, consider a diverse range of ideas, challenge business as usual, and engage in productive debate – and simultaneously to reduce the *social friction* that impedes the feeling of belonging, inclusiveness and support within the team.

How do we do this in practice? Clark proposes a compelling model, suggesting that psychological safety is contingent on the level of respect and permission members feel.

When respect is high but permission is low, for example, group dynamics are cordial but the culture is paternalistic. People are either told what to do or their ideas are humoured but seldom actioned, and as a consequence team members become leader-dependent or leave in frustration. By contrast, where permission is high but respect is low, the culture becomes exploitative. Team members treated as disposable by despotic leaders on a quest for glory tend to leave for the sake of their own sanity. Respect and permission are therefore both essential and must be kept in balance.

According to Clark, respect and permission grow as a team passes through four levels of safety. First comes *inclusion safety* – the basic feeling of acceptance and belonging within the group, without which we don't really feel part of the team at all. The second level is *learner safety*, where we feel encouraged to ask questions and experiment, and supported if we make mistakes. Third is *contributor safety*, where we are granted more autonomy as we demonstrate our abilities. And finally we have *challenger safety* – we begin to feel comfortable challenging the status quo without the risk of punishment.[18] Each stage builds on the previous one to unlock the team's fullest potential.

As I studied this model I was struck by how profoundly these levels of safety affect not just the performance of project teams, but our quality of life more broadly. I think of one leader who dragged me into the corridor outside a meeting room and mauled me for questioning them in front of their colleagues. I think of the times great ideas were ignored because of who or where they came from. I think of friends who don't feel that basic inclusion safety at work because of the colour of their skin. I think of another smart friend who can hardly motivate himself to participate in meetings because nothing ever changes; nobody can question the way things are done, so nothing can improve.

I think of the millions of dollars I've seen wasted over the years because people feel uncomfortable either admitting that mistakes have been made or challenging a flawed course of action. And I think of the teams who felt unable to contribute to the success of their organisation because their CEO hoarded decision-making power and micro-managed their every move.

The waste of time, energy, talent and other resources is tragic, and I can't help but consider the broader ramifications too – for education, parenting, and other activities where team-work is crucial to success.

That said, I also think how fortunate I have been to have worked in teams where those forms of psychological safety are deeply ingrained, where the right dynamics have been swiftly put in place – and the sense of fulfilment that has ensued.

Leaders must set the tone from the top, creating an inclusive environment, encouraging learning, delegating effectively to maximise contributions, and welcoming challenging ideas. The more chaotic the environment in which the business operates, the more important these factors become. When decision-making power is concentrated at the top, fast-moving events can overwhelm leaders, who have trained their team members not to think and act for themselves – a lethal combination.

Dov Charney, the founder of American Apparel, makes for an extreme case study. From day one he decided he would be a hyper-accessible leader. Anybody – employees, customers, suppliers or journalists – could contact him directly. He was at the centre of every aspect of the business. According to an account by Ryan Holiday – the bestselling author and former marketing director at American Apparel – this served Charney well in the early days, but as the business scaled to 250 stores in twenty countries it became toxic. By 2014 he was responding to a deluge of requests from every corner of the globe and had all but stopped sleeping. Unsurprisingly, his judgement suffered.

Desperate to fix a bungled shift between distribution facilities, he moved into the warehouse, putting a bed in a small office, which only made matters worse. His decision-making became increasingly erratic, confused and contradictory until eventually his mother was called to take him home. Within a year he was out of his job, the company had collapsed and he owed a hedge fund $20 million.[19]

Instead of hoarding decision-making power for themselves, leaders should empower their employees to decide the means by which their visions might be achieved, and emphasise the value of learning and adaptability.

Ritz Carlton Hotels, for example, have a clear credo: to be 'a place where the genuine care and comfort of our guests is our highest mission'. To this end their staff are empowered to spend up to $2,000 on a guest should they spot an opportunity to do something exceptional.[20]

In a similar vein, employees within some companies – most notably tech giants such as Google and Atlassian – are encouraged to explore their own ideas, spending as much as twenty per cent of their work time pursuing their own initiatives, a stratagem that echoes some of our earlier themes. They do not know what the payoff from these personal projects might be, but a single great idea is worth the reduced productivity: *exploratory growth* and *affordable loss* in action.

William Thorndike Jr's analysis of the working practices of unusually successful CEOs, *The Outsiders*, found yet more support for creating a culture where people feel contributor safety and permission to take action. He discovered that CEOs who massively outperform the market favour a radically decentralised structure, with a flat management profile and emphasis on individual autonomy.

In the words of Warren Buffett, to *release entrepreneurial energy* within their businesses they aim to 'Hire well (and) manage little'.[21] But what does hiring well look like? Ability and attitude are not to be overlooked, of course, but another ingredient can be just as important: *diversity*.

The benefits of diversity

There are two basic forms of diversity we must consider: demographic and cognitive. Demographic diversity involves such factors as race, gender, age, socio-economic status and educational background. Cognitive diversity involves differences in what we do and how we do it. Let's start there.

How can we differ cognitively? At the highest level we can have diverse preferences – goals and values, essentially – but we can also have diverse means of approaching those goals: the perspectives and problem-solving approaches that constitute our particular intellectual toolkit.[22] But how does cognitive diversity actually help our performance?

Again, we can think of this as a numbers game. The more perspectives, skills or decision-making heuristics the team has at their disposal, the more potential solutions to problems it has, and the more chance there is of a breakthrough innovation when those resources are pooled. This makes intuitive sense – if everyone had the same mental models and skills there'd be no benefit to having a team, except to increase capacity.

When problems are particularly challenging, the people all smart, and the team size sufficiently large (more than a handful at least), diversity can further improve our performance.[23] It can even trump raw ability. If all of our smartest people try to solve a problem using the same tools, they can all get stuck in the same place.[24]

As Chapter 3 explained, to thrive in uncertain conditions we must have a *truth-seeking* mindset – a willingness to recalibrate our beliefs in response to valuable new information gained through active open-mindedness, seeking multiple perspectives, and avoiding attachment to one big idea. Another recurring theme in the book is the need to deviate from the consensus – to avoid being too similar to others in thought patterns and worldview if we're looking to outperform our rivals.

With these considerations in mind, it's clear that a cognitively homogeneous team is a handicap in an uncertain world. It amplifies confirmation bias, limits our access to information, narrows our scope of opportunity and causes us to converge on a consensus worldview. If everyone is looking in the same direction, we're perilously exposed to unexpected events hurtling towards us from the periphery.[25]

As the computer pioneer Alan Kay remarked, 'A change in perspective is worth eighty IQ points.'[26] By purposefully creating teams of diverse individuals we supercharge our ability to spot new opportunities, generate unusual ideas, consider challenges from different angles, manage risks and avoid the dreaded *groupthink*. Or as Jacob Bronowski put it: 'Diversity is the propeller of evolution.'[27]

What of demographic diversity, though? Is there any benefit to hiring people with different identities and backgrounds? The answer is an unequivocal yes.

Aside from the obvious and urgent moral imperative to overcome discrimination and misrepresentation within corporations and society at large, demographic diversity can increase performance because it tends to go hand in hand with cognitive diversity.[28]

Our different backgrounds and experiences give us different perspectives, different mental models and different approaches to problem-solving. However, we can only take advantage of these differences if we work together effectively. Diversity and psychological safety are therefore inextricably linked. The potential benefits of hiring a diverse workforce cannot be realised without inclusion safety, for example – a feeling of belonging and acceptance. And the benefits of a psychologically safe environment can be amplified by increasing diversity.

And while achieving both is not a simple matter – ironically Google has a way to go on handling racism and sexual harassment, according to an opinion piece in the *New York Times* – what could possibly be more worthy of tenacious, long-term commitment, given the benefits that will accrue both in the workplace and in society at large?[29] Many individuals understandably feel jaded by bad experiences, we still have a lot to learn, and the path ahead is indeed long and challenging, but it is undeniably worth taking.

The advantage of generalism

As an organisation grows, its workforce becomes more specialised to take advantage of deeper subject matter expertise, and these specialists are then organised into some kind of divisional structure – typically by discipline, business unit or both.

The problem, as I explained at the start of the book, is that these divisions are to a large extent artificial. A business is a dynamic system, where a change in one area will affect the others; it's an interconnected whole, where success is determined not by the performance of each individual department but by how well the activities of various departments are coordinated.

A real-world example from a workshop we facilitated demonstrates this principle in action.

The CEO of a fast-growing distribution business thought they could improve their customer experience by making it easier to return unused or unwanted products, so we put together a group of people from across the company – customer service, logistics, legal, accounting and operations – to evaluate the idea.

The customer service representative was strongly in favour of the project. People often complained about the returns policy, expectations were rising, and the customer is always right, they argued. The person from logistics, however, looked incredulous. She pointed out that there was literally no room in the warehouse to store any more products, so the policy change would be impossible to execute without expanding capacity at vast cost. She issued a stark ultimatum: kill the project or buy an extra warehouse.

Their exchanges were getting progressively more heated until the person from legal piped up. 'It's strange . . . I'd have thought the reason customers were unhappy is because we have six or seven different return policies which are not consistently enforced. If we had just one simpler policy that was better communicated we might not need to change the terms at all. We could take the rough edge off the customer experience without necessarily increasing the volume of returns.'

The customer service and logistics representatives looked at her in surprise. Because both had considered the issue only from their own perspectives, neither had given any thought as to whether the problem might actually have its origins elsewhere.

This realisation led to a solution everyone could get behind: by consolidating down to a single clearly explained and enforced returns policy, the company would be able to improve its customer experience and simplify its operations, without the cost of expanding their capacity.

What can we do to make this kind of coordination easier? The first step is to broaden people's general understanding of how a business actually functions. Increasing levels of financial literacy within a company – a basic understanding of concepts like cost structure, cash flow and working capital, for example – should improve decision-making overall because each individual will have a better sense of how their work affects the financial performance of the company.

The second step is to foster a greater understanding of other fields of work. If design, customer service and marketing had a deeper appreciation for each other's disciplines, for example, they would find it easier to integrate their various activities for the good of the customer, brand and company as a whole.

General business knowledge also serves us well as we become more senior or decide to launch our own venture. In fact, one of the greatest benefits of starting your own business is that regardless of how successful it becomes, you come to appreciate all the moving parts of an enterprise that must be brought into harmony.

It's amazing, for example, how quickly people go from trash-talking marketing activities like advertising or PR that aim to build awareness, to becoming obsessed with them when they start their own business. As ad-man David Droga wittily remarked, 'Everyone hates advertising until they want to sell their house or find their missing cat.'[30]

Yet the matter of generalism vs specialism, and the attendant realisation that poor coordination can be a bigger impediment to performance than technical competence, begs another question: how should we structure our operations and teams to thrive in our unpredictable, uncertain environment?

The power of adaptability

We cannot thrive in the face of uncertainty if the spirit is strong but the flesh is weak. It's not much help having the right mindset and culture if the infrastructure of the business cannot respond to change. Yet in practice many businesses are over-optimised, and paralysed by process and protocol.

Given the choice between maintaining their ability to adapt or operating more efficiently, most elect to remove slack from the system since it gives a quantifiable short-term gain. By contrast, adaptability is a bit like insurance – seemingly wasteful until you need it, at which point you really need it. Over time, then, organisations become dragsters – unbeatable in a straight line but unable to handle the simplest bump in the road, let alone a sharp corner.[31] And while efficiency is desirable in routine, stable environments with standardised processes, innovation – which requires experimentation, tinkering, and trial and error – is inherently inefficient, as are methods of building social capital and strengthening relationships. Exploratory growth – the source of our future opportunities – is also inherently inefficient compared to exploiting existing ones.

In other words, most of the things that have the greatest upside – innovating, building high-quality relationships and discovering massive growth opportunities – cannot be done efficiently. And by extending Taylorist methods and mentalities to domains that are inherently inefficient, we compromise rather than amplify our success. 'Strategy,' wrote Jules Goddard in *Uncommon Sense, Common Nonsense*, 'is the rare and precious skill of staying one step ahead of the need to be efficient.'[32]

Adaptability is therefore paramount, particularly during the nascent stages of an idea. We do not know at the start whether we'll need to scale up, change direction or kill a project altogether. It is only when we establish and test our foothold in the market that we should begin to entertain serious notions about improving efficiency.

New ideas are weak and fragile things, though. They are easily killed, especially if they challenge norms or must compete for resources and attention with today's top performers, or are expected to produce results immediately. We therefore need to go a step beyond basic adaptability and put specific structures in place to protect and nurture them – the topic I'll turn to now.

Loonshots and franchises

It has always interested me how little relationship there seems to be between inventiveness and resources.

How is it, for example, that the most innovative motorcycle of all time was designed and built in a New Zealand shed by one man, who then schooled manufacturers' teams at races around the world?[33] He even made the engine from scratch. And why are startups seemingly able to pursue breakthrough new ideas so much more easily than most large corporations, despite their lesser means and greater individual risk exposure? It can't be a matter of the people themselves, since many people quit their jobs at big companies to join startups and vice versa. If individual risk appetite or enthusiasm for new ideas was the problem we'd never see this kind of cross-pollination.

After years of idle curiosity, rumination and study, the closest I've seen to a compelling answer comes from the physicist and biotech entrepreneur Safi Bahcall, whose explanation draws on his knowledge of both domains.

According to Bahcall, the ability to nurture breakthrough new ideas – what he calls 'loonshots' – and the skill to build on existing successes – or 'franchises' – is akin to phases of matter. Just as water cannot be liquid and solid simultaneously, an organisation's structure, incentives and management cannot simultaneously be optimised for inventing the imaginative new products of the future, and exploiting existing market opportunities in the present.

However, when water moves from liquid to solid it undergoes a phase transition where at an exact temperature blocks of ice form within pools of water. The two phases coexist, together but separate, in dynamic equilibrium. One degree either way and it totally freezes or melts.

Bahcall finds the same logic of phase transitions applies to organisations, where certain managerial parameters can shift incentives towards supporting either loonshots or franchises, or achieve that miraculous equilibrium state where both are possible. How does this work in practice?

The primary variables at work are the two competing forces of *stake* and *rank*.[34] In a small startup, for example, if our loonshot idea overcomes the odds to succeed, we all stand to become extremely wealthy. We all have a high stake in the success of the venture in other words, and with just a handful of people in the company there are no benefits to rank.

At some point, however, if our startup succeeds it will reach a size where the perks of rank become equal. Given the choice between supporting a crazy idea that has a high risk of failure, might take years to come to fruition and won't make much of a difference to our personal success if it does, and backing a franchise project that is more likely to succeed and result in a promotion or pay rise within a year, the obvious choice is to dismiss the crazy idea and stick to the knitting. The organisation has undergone a phase transition.

As Bahcall explains, though, this transition point can be

adjusted by manipulating managerial factors that shift an individual's incentives towards project work or politics. Five factors warrant particular consideration.

First there is the *management span* – the number of direct reports under any one level of the hierarchy. The wider this span, the fewer opportunities there are for promotion, so the less the incentive to play politics. When spans are wider, we're also more likely to share ideas and seek feedback from our peers – a better structure for encouraging experimentation and innovation.

Next we have the *salary step up* and our *equity fraction*. The bigger the step up between levels of the hierarchy, the more incentivised we are to focus on rank; the smaller the step, the more we'll focus on project work. And the more equity we have, the more we'll focus on the commercial success of the business.

Finally, we have two subtler fitness factors: *project-skill fit* and *return on politics*. If we're exceptionally skilled at our job, enjoy it, and can have an obvious positive impact on a project's outcome, we're naturally more likely to focus our attention on the work itself than if we're stuck in a role where we can't contribute much. Similarly, if office politics seems to be a decisive factor in who makes their way up the greasy pole – as opposed to the quality of their project work – you can bet that's where people's efforts will go.[35]

By manipulating these factors, we can tune people's incentives towards stake or rank, and with that their support of loonshots or franchise plays. A better approach, arguably, is to separate these organisations entirely, creating a loonshot nursery dedicated to nurturing bold new ideas outside of the franchise business.

My own experience, however, has taught me that separating

the organisations on paper is not necessarily enough to separate their mentalities, especially if cues in the environment and operations are carried over from the mothership.

I once worked with an innovation lab that had been blessed with the most lavish offices I've ever seen, and whose team members spent an inordinate amount of time flying around the world in business class to visit prospective partners.

There was something about the sheer sense of abundance that pervaded the operation – from the marble entrance and designer furniture to the perks, budgets and staffing – that meant there was none of the sense of urgency or excitement that you usually find in startups, where the prospect of failure is ever present, and your little gang has banded together to take a voyage into the unknown. It's hard not to feel like you've already arrived as you gaze out of your corner office with your rump firmly planted in an Eames chair. Needless to say, this particular organisation spent a lot and achieved very little. It was fun while it lasted, though.

In stark contrast, independent startups tend to have very limited resources, the smallest teams possible, and their physical environment – if they even have an office – tends to be low-key. There are plenty of stories, for example, of tech companies that started life in a garage, or founders assembling their own IKEA furniture on day one. Lockheed's Skunk Works, the prototypical startup-within-a-big-company, built their first aeroplane in a tent.

I've always believed that constraints such as these play as much of a role in our success as resources do. Limitations – whether of time, money or personnel – unlock our creativity. They force us to prioritise, focus and improvise, and a sense of scarcity discourages complacency. For our nursery to succeed, then, it's important that the separation between the franchise and nursery extends beyond basic organisational structure and incentives, and into operations, resources and environment.

Another challenge comes when a concept makes its way out of the nursery and into the franchise so that it can enter the market. If the transfer is too forced – pushed on the franchise by an enthusiastic leader – the risk is that vital insights from those in the franchise are ignored. If the transfer is too weak, promising ideas will never gain the attention of the franchise, who are incentivised to exploit existing opportunities. Balance is essential.[36]

In order to manage this transition, it is vital that both groups – the *artists and soldiers* as Bahcall calls them – are equally respected by the organisation, and that the transfer is carefully managed with the help of project champions who are not only familiar with both sides and can bridge the two, but are also skilled at internal sales.[37]

'The weak link,' writes Bahcall, 'is not the supply of ideas. It is the transfer to the field. And underlying that weak link is structure – the design of the system – rather than the people or the culture.'

Fortunately, structure is something that, unlike culture, can be directly manipulated, as can the other factors we've addressed in this chapter: how we set goals and use metrics, who we hire, and how they are trained to make decisions.

We cannot wave a magic wand and transform an organisation overnight, but with patience and commitment we can build more diverse teams, increase their psychological safety, and provide them with the incentives and environments they need to flourish, whatever wildness lies in wait.

Chapter summary

- How people are hired, managed and incentivised, and how teams are structured, affects an organisation's ability to thrive under uncertainty.
- Although goals are fundamentally helpful, they can be destructive when fixed goals come into conflict with the unpredictable nature of our environment.
- In uncertain environments it is better to focus on learning goals than performance goals.
- Metric fixation can create perverse incentives and be a catalyst for destructive goal pursuit.
- An obsession with metrics discourages risk-taking and innovation.
- In organisations with a negative error culture, decision-making becomes defensive, and the ability to adapt, learn and grow is compromised. A positive error culture has the opposite effect.
- A primary task of leaders is to create an environment where intellectual friction increases and social friction decreases.
- Psychological safety is a crucial determinant of team performance and an organisation's ability to thrive amid uncertainty.
- There are four stages of psychological safety: inclusion safety, learning safety, contributor safety and challenger safety.
- Cognitive diversity increases the likelihood of breakthrough innovations and helps us solve problems more effectively by creating a bigger toolkit to work with.
- Demographic and cognitive diversity go hand in hand.
- Diversity and psychological safety are tightly coupled. Without psychological safety a diverse team will not perform

well. A psychologically safe environment will benefit from greater diversity.

- General business skills are a powerful addition to specialist domain expertise, improving communication and decision-making.
- Organisations must remain adaptable and acknowledge that many activities that are most beneficial to a business are inherently inefficient.
- Whether a team focuses on nurturing breakthrough ideas or exploiting existing market opportunities depends on their individual incentives.
- Organisations should create separate but integrated structures for nurturing new ideas and franchises, and carefully manage the back-and-forth between the two.

Afterword

You can't write a book about chance and success without re-assessing a little of your own history in the process. Retracing my steps with a deeper appreciation for randomness, serendipity, and the cognitive and cultural forces that obscure them, I see past events in an altogether different light.

I could not have known when I boarded that train to Oxford, for example, that leafing through a discarded newspaper would set my career in motion. And as I unpacked my laptop on the first day of a consulting gig back in 2007, I had no idea that I'd end up running a business on the other side of the world with the stranger sitting next to me.

Csaba tells me he had no intention of attending the party where we first met, but decided to go at the last minute. Without that snap decision – and the unforeseeable course of events that led me to be there too – we would not have written this book and you would not have read it.

As I reflect on these chance encounters, I am struck, in particular, by their absurd triviality. Life-changing events have never been obvious in the moment. A single grain of rice has just gently bumped another in the pile.

These instances remind me of Kurt Vonnegut's advice to 'Enjoy the little things in life because one day you'll look back and realise they were the big things.' The next small encounter

with a stranger may be the beginning of a life-changing part-
nership. A minor frustration with a product or service could
birth a great enterprise. And history teaches us that great breakthroughs are more often born of chance encounters, happy
accidents and curious tinkering than rigorous, logical analysis.

So while there is no way to eliminate uncertainty from our
environment, neither should we want to. And if we subscribe
to Seneca's belief that luck is what happens when preparation
meets opportunity, then there is plenty we can do to be better
prepared and create more opportunity: from the mindset we
adopt and the relationships we develop, to the strategies we
pursue and the team structures we create.

Just as importantly, we can find greater happiness, ease and
excitement by embracing rather than fighting the unpredictability of our surroundings. A greater sense of control over
outcomes will not come from futile attempts to banish uncertainty, but from making that uncertainty work in our favour. To
paraphrase Aristotle Onassis, we cannot command the ocean
to do our bidding, but we can learn to sail through weather fair
or foul, and need never stop exploring.

If you've enjoyed the book, have applied these concepts in
practice and would like to share your stories, we would love to
hear from you – especially if you think there is an opportunity
to collaborate via Tiller Partners or Methodical. Please email
authors@mastering-uncertainty.com.

Who knows where it might lead. After all, what's your
downside?

Notes

Introduction

1. Myers, T.W., *Anatomy Trains* (London: Elsevier, 2009), 22.
2. http://news.bbc.co.uk/2/hi/business/3704669.stm
3. Haidt, J., *The Righteous Mind* (New York: Pantheon Books, 2012), ch. 3.

1. Chance encounters

1. Chesterton, G.K., *Orthodoxy* (Digireads.com Publishing, 2018), 55.
2. https://www.olympic.org/news/steven-bradbury-australia-s-last-man-standing
3. Trivers, R., *The Folly of Fools: The Logic of Deceit and Self-Deception in Human Life* (New York: Basic Books, 2011), ch. 1.
4. Bernstein, P.L., *Against the Gods* (New York: John Wiley & Sons, 1998), 232.
5. Marks, H., *Mastering the Market Cycle – Getting the Odds on Your Side* (New York: Houghton Mifflin Harcourt, 2018), 138.
6. Kordupleski, R. and Simpson, J., *Mastering Customer Value Management – The Art and Science of Creating Competitive Advantage* (Randolph, NJ: Customer Value Management, Inc.), xvi–xvii.
7. Buchanan, M., *Ubiquity: Why Catastrophes Happen* (New York: Three Rivers Press, 2000), 46.

8. Taleb, N.N., *The Black Swan: The Impact of the Highly Improbable* (New York: Random House, 2010), 15.

9. Ibid., 39.

10. Arthur, W.B., *Complexity and the Economy* (Oxford: Oxford University Press, 2014), ch. 2.

11. Reason, J., *Managing the Risk of Organisational Accidents* (Abingdon: Taylor & Francis, 2016), 11.

12. Ibid., 74.

13. Arthur, W.B., *The Nature of Technology: What It Is and How It Evolves* (New York: The Free Press, 2011; Kindle edn), 33.

14. Ibid., 103.

15. Yes, really. See Seaborg, G.T., *A Scientist Speaks Out: A Personal Perspective on Science, Society and Change* (London: World Scientific Publishing, 1996), 217.

16. Livingston, J., *Founders at Work* (Berkeley: Apress, 2007), 284.

17. In Amazon's 2016 letter to shareholders, Jeff Bezos wrote, 'Outsized returns often come from betting against conventional wisdom, and conventional wisdom is usually right. Given a ten percent chance of a 100 times payoff, you should take that bet every time. But you're still going to be wrong nine times out of ten . . . We all know that if you swing for the fences, you're going to strike out a lot, but you're also going to hit some home runs. The difference between baseball and business, however, is that baseball has a truncated outcome distribution. When you swing, no matter how well you connect with the ball, the most runs you can get is four. In business, every once in a while, when you step up to the plate, you can score 1,000 runs. This long-tailed distribution of returns is why it's important to be bold. Big winners pay for so many experiments.' Accessed at: https://www.sec.gov/Archives/edgar/data/1018724/000119312516530910/d168744dex991.htm

18. https://blog.aboutamazon.com/company-news/2018-letter-to-shareholders

19. Marks, H., *The Value of Predictions, or Where'd All This Rain Come From?* (Los Angeles: Oaktree Capital Management, L.P., 1993).

2. Standing in Taylor's shadow

1. Graeber, D., *Bullshit Jobs* (New York: Simon & Schuster, 2018), 83.
2. Tetlock, P.E. and Gardner, D., *Superforecasting* (New York: Crown Publishing Group, 2015), 96.
3. Redding, A.C., *Google It: A History of Google* (New York: Feiwel and Friends, 2018), ch. 4.
4. Hatfield has recounted the story in various documentaries and interviews, including *Respect the Architects: The Paris Air Max 1 Story*.
5. https://www.rollingstone.com/culture/culture-news/how-spider-man-conquered-the-world-189368/
6. https://www.cultofmac.com/383779/leica-invented-autofocus-then-abandoned-it/
7. Dobelli, R., *The Art of Thinking Clearly* (London: Hodder & Stoughton, 2013), 119.
8. https://www.quantamagazine.org/to-make-sense-of-the-present-brains-may-predict-the-future-20180710/
9. Rosenzweig, P., *The Halo Effect* (New York: Free Press, 2007), 74.
10. Ibid., ch. 4.
11. Kahneman, D., *Thinking, Fast and Slow* (London: Allen Lane, 2011), 425.
12. Ibid., ch. 12.
13. Frank, R.H., *Success and Luck: Good Fortune and the Myth of Meritocracy* (Princeton: Princeton University Press, 2016), 79–82.
14. Perroni, A.G. and Wrege, C.D., 'Taylor's Pig-Tale: A Historical Analysis of Frederick W. Taylor's Pig-Iron Experiments' (*Academy of Management Journal*, Vol. 17, No. 1, Mar. 1974), 6–27.

15. Kiechel, W., *The Lords of Strategy: The Secret Intellectual History of the New Corporate World* (Boston: Harvard Business School Press, 2010), ch. 1.

16. https://aeropress.com/pages/about

17. Bhide, A.V., *Origin and Evolution of New Business* (New York: Oxford University Press, 2000).

18. Marks, H., *Dare to be Great* (Los Angeles: Oaktree Capital Management, L.P., 2006).

19. Popper, K.R., *The Logic of Scientific Discovery* (London: Routledge Classics, 2002), 18.

20. Rosenzweig, P., *The Halo Effect* (New York: Free Press, 2007), 84–93.

21. Clayman, M., 'In Search of Excellence: The Investor's Viewpoint' (*Financial Analysts Journal*, Vol. 43, No. 3, 1987) 54–63. JSTOR, www.jstor.org/stable/4479032. Accessed 17 Nov. 2020.

22. This is BCG's own account of events. See: https://web.archive.org/web/20130204055506/http://www.bcg.com/about_bcg/history/history_1965.aspx

23. Stewart, M., *The Management Myth* (New York: W.W. Norton & Company, 2009), 195.

24. O'Shea, J. and Madigan, C., *Dangerous Company: The Consulting Powerhouses and the Businesses They Save and Ruin* (New York: Times Books, 1997), 154.

25. https://www.drucker.institute/perspective/about-peter-drucker/

26. Henry Mintzberg's book *Strategy Safari* provides an excellent overview of each of these schools of strategic thought. See Mintzberg, H., Ahlstrand, B. and Lampel, J., *Strategy Safari: A Guided Tour Through the Wilds of Strategic Management* (New York: The Free Press, 1998).

27. Martin, R., *Playing to Win: How Strategy Really Works* (Boston: Harvard Business School Publishing, 2013).

28. The ranking is according to Thinkers50, which rated the authors as the world's top business thinkers in 2019. They also gave *Blue Ocean Strategy* their 2011 Strategy Award for 'the business book of the decade'. See https://thinkers50.com/biographies/w-chan-kim-renee-mauborgne/

29. Lowe, J., *Jack Welch Speaks: Wit and Wisdom from the World's Greatest Business Leader* (Hoboken: John Wiley & Sons, 2008), 90.

30. Mintzberg, H., Pascale, R.T., Goold, M. and Rumelt, R.P., 'The "Honda Effect" Revisited' (*California Management Review*, Vol. 38, No. 4, 1996), 78–91.

31. I'm grateful to strategist J.P. Castlin for sharing this insight with me.

32. Hacking, I., *The Taming of Chance (Ideas in Context)* (Cambridge: Cambridge University Press, 1990).

33. Bahcall, S., *Loonshots* (New York: St. Martin's Press, 2019), 19.

34. https://www.sciencealert.com/these-eighteen-accidental-scientific-discoveries-changed-the-world

35. Bacon, F., *The Advancement of Learning* (Public domain), 28.

3. *A matter of mindset*

1. https://ramp.space/en/post/team-player-rafael-nadal

2. https://www.telegraph.co.uk/sport/tennis/rafaelnadal/8707878/Rafael-Nadal-Uncle-Toni-terrified-me-but-without-him-Id-be-nothing.html

3. https://www.technologyreview.com/2018/03/01/144958/if-youre-so-smart-why-arent-you-rich-turns-out-its-just-chance/

4. Baumeister, R.F., Bratslavsky, E., Finkenauer, C. and VohsBad, K.D., 'Bad is Stronger than Good' (*Review of General Psychology*, Vol. 5, Issue 4, 2001), 323–370.

5. Dyer, F.L. and Martin, T.C., *Edison: His Life and Inventions* (New York: Harper & Brothers, 1910), Vol. 2, 615–616.

6. Jordan, M., *I Can't Accept Not Trying: Michael Jordan on the Pursuit of Excellence* (San Francisco: Harper, 1994), 12.

7. This famous quote first appeared in the 16 January 1983 edition of *The Hockey News*. Gretzky made the remark in response to editor Bob McKenzie's comment that he had taken a lot of shots that year.

8. See *Oakley* (New York: Assouline Publishing, 2014), Heritage. Also: https://www.forbes.com/2007/06/21/luxottica-oakley-update-markets-equity-cx_vr_0621markets21.html?sh=60f031e33896

9. Sarasvathy, S.D., *Effectuation: Elements of Entrepreneurial Expertise* (Northampton, MA: Edward Elgar, 2008), 34, 81–83, 88, 115.

10. Dweck, C.S., *Mindset: The New Psychology of Success* (New York: Random House, 2016), ch. 1.

11. https://www.linkedin.com/pulse/satya-nadella-growth-mindsets-learn-it-all-does-better-jessi-hempel/

12. Editorial contribution and arrangement by Langworth, R.M., *Churchill by Himself: The Definitive Collection of Quotations* (London: Ebury Press, 2008).

13. Duckworth, A., *Grit: The Power of Passion and Perseverance* (New York: Scribner, 2016), 25.

14. https://www.theguardian.com/books/2015/mar/24/jk-rowling-tells-fans-twitter-loads-rejections-before-harry-potter-success

15. Nathan, J., *Sony* (New York: Houghton Mifflin Company, 1990), 13.

16. Dyson, J., *Against the Odds: An Autobiography* (London: Orion Business, 1997).

17. Duckworth, A., *Grit: The Power of Passion and Perseverance* (New York: Scribner, 2016), 92.

18. Reisman, D., Glazer, N. and Denney, R., *The Lonely Crowd* (London: Yale University Press, 2001), 24–25.

19. Glubb, J., *The Fate of Empires and Search for Survival* (Edinburgh: William Blackwood & Sons, 1976), 14.

20. The footballer Cristiano Ronaldo, singer Ariana Grande, and actor Dwayne Johnson.

21. Reisman, D., Glazer, N. and Denney, R., *The Lonely Crowd* (London: Yale University Press, 2001), 190.

22. Appiah, K.A., *The Lies That Bind: Rethinking Identity* (New York: Liveright Publishing, 2018), 9.

23. Clear, J., *Atomic Habits* (New York: Avery, 2018), 36.

24. Gross, M., *Genuine Authentic: The Real Life of Ralph Lauren* (New York: Harper Collins, 2003), 2.

25. Ibid., xvii.

26. If these examples tickle you, I highly recommend the source material: Currey, M., *Daily Rituals* (New York: Alfred A. Knopf, 2013).

27. https://www.sciencedaily.com/releases/2020/06/200630111504. htm

28. Bartlett, J. and O'Brien, G., *Bartlett's Familiar Quotations* (New York: Little, Brown, and Company, 2012), 707.

29. Newport. C., *Deep Work: Rules for Focused Success in a Distracted World* (New York: Hachette, 2016).

30. Duke, A., *Thinking in Bets* (New York: Portfolio/Penguin, 2018).

31. Tetlock, P.E. and Gardner, D., *Superforecasting* (New York: Crown Publishing Group, 2015), 191.

32. Pollan, M., *How to Change Your Mind* (New York: Penguin Press, 2018), ch. 1.

33. Isaacson, W., *Steve Jobs* (London: Little, Brown, 2011), 501.

34. https://www.apple.com/newsroom/2020/06/apples-app-store-ecosystem-facilitated-over-half-a-trillion-dollars-in-commerce-in-2019/

35. The quote is most often attributed to Frank Lloyd Wright, although it is disputed. *The Yale Book of Quotations* instead references Will Rogers, who reportedly said, 'Tilt this country on end and everything loose will slide into Los Angeles' in the 17 May 1964 edition of the *Washington Post*. See Shapiro,

F.R., *The Yale Book of Quotations* (New Haven: Yale University Press, 2006), 841.

36. Both Annie Duke and Angela Duckworth make similar points in their books. See: Duke, A., *Thinking in Bets* (New York: Portfolio/Penguin, 2018), ch. 4.; and Duckworth, A., *Grit: The Power of Passion and Perseverance* (New York: Scribner, 2016), 246.
37. Greene, R., *Mastery* (New York: Penguin Books, 2013), 2–3.
38. Ibid., ch. 1.
39. While not a direct quotation from Victor Frankl's seminal book *Man's Search for Meaning,* it is close enough in spirit to be worthy of attribution. See Frankl, V.E., *Man's Search for Meaning* (Boston: Beacon Books, 2006) and http://www.logotherapyinstitute.org/About_Logotherapy.html

4. *Social capital*

1. Livingston, J., *Founders at Work* (Berkeley: Apress, 2007), 1.
2. Isaacson, W., *Steve Jobs* (London: Little, Brown, 2011), 431.
3. Buchanan, M., *Nexus: Small Worlds and the Groundbreaking Science of Networks* (New York: W.W. Norton & Company, 2002) and Watts, D.J., *Small Worlds: The Dynamics of Networks Between Order and Randomness* (Princeton: Princeton University Press, 2018).
4. Mill, J.S., *On Liberty* (New York: Dover Publications, Inc., 2002), 80.
5. See Axelrod, R., *The Evolution of Cooperation* (Cambridge: Basic Books, 1984) for an explanation of the relationship between what Axelrod calls 'The Shadow of the Future' and the nature of cooperation.
6. Trivers, R.L., 'The Evolution of Reciprocal Altruism' (*Quarterly Review of Biology,* Vol. 46, 1971), 35–57.
7. Stewart-Williams, S., *The Ape That Understood the Universe* (Cambridge: Cambridge University Press, 2018), 192.

8. Sun, L., *The Fairness Instinct: The Robin Hood Mentality and our Biological Nature* (New York: Prometheus Books, 2013), 32.

9. Zahavi, A. and Zahavi, A., *The Handicap Principle – A Missing Piece of Darwin's Puzzle* (Oxford: Oxford University Press).

10. Ibid., ch. 10.

11. Sutherland, R., *Alchemy – The Surprising Power of Ideas That Don't Make Sense* (London: WH Allen, 2019), ch. 3.4.

12. Keltner, D., *The Power Paradox* (New York: Penguin Press, 2014), 70.

13. Bahcall, S., *Loonshots* (New York: St. Martin's Press, 2019), 8.

14. https://www.codusoperandi.com/posts/increasing-your-luck-surface-area

15. Busch, C., *The Serendipity Mindset* (New York: Riverhead Books, 2020), 146.

16. Stewart-Williams, S., *The Ape That Understood the Universe* (Cambridge: Cambridge University Press, 2018), 196.

17. http://www.jonahlehrer.com/2013/02/my-apology

18. https://newrepublic.com/article/112416/jonah-lehrers-20000-apology-wasnt-enough

19. Watkinson, M., *The Ten Principles Behind Great Customer Experiences* (Harlow: FT Press, 2013), ch. 7.

5. Selling

1. Cope, M., *The Seven Cs of Consulting* (Harlow: FT Prentice Hall, 2003), 103.

2. Keenan, J., *Gap Selling* (Jim Keenan, 2018).

3. Blount, J., *Fanatical Prospecting* (Hoboken: John Wiley & Sons, Inc., 2015), 31.

4. Keenan suggests capturing this in a *Problem Identification Chart*. See Keenan, J., *Gap Selling* (Jim Keenan, 2018), ch. 2.

5. Dixon, M. and Adamson, B., *The Challenger Sale: Taking Control of the Customer Conversation* (New York: Portfolio/Penguin, 2011).

6. Blount, J., *Fanatical Prospecting* (Hoboken: John Wiley & Sons, Inc., 2015), 147.

7. Keenan, J., *Gap Selling* (Jim Keenan, 2018), ch. 17.

8. Rackham, N., *Spin Selling* (New York: McGraw Hill Education, 2017), 48.

9. Kline, N., *Time to Think* (London: Octopus Publishing Group, 1999), ch. 3.

10. Gerber, M., *The E Myth Revisited* (New York: HarperCollins eBooks, 2009), 118.

11. Rackham, N., *Spin Selling* (New York: McGraw Hill Education, 2017).

12. I discovered the term 'entry trick' in Robert Twigger's book *Micromastery*. See Twigger, R., *Micromastery: Learn small, learn fast and unlock your potential to achieve anything* (London: Tarcher Perigee, 2017), 8.

13. Minto, B., *The Pyramid Principle* (Harlow: Pearson Education Limited, 2009), ch. 4.

14. Ibid., ch. 1.

15. Matt Dixon makes a similar point in *The Challenger Sale* – suggesting these words be removed from presentation material altogether. See Dixon, M. and Adamson, B., *The Challenger Sale: Taking Control of the Customer Conversation* (New York: Portfolio/Penguin, 2011), ch. 9.

16. Watkinson, M., *The Grid: The Master Model Behind Business Success* (London: Random House, 2017), 194.

17. Reynolds, N., *We Have a Deal: How to negotiate with intelligence, flexibility and power* (London: Icon Books, 2016), 84–87.

18. Kahneman, D., *Thinking, Fast and Slow* (London: Allen Lane, 2011), 119.

19. Reynolds, N., *We Have a Deal: How to negotiate with intelligence, flexibility and power* (London: Icon Books, 2016), 60–69.

20. Ibid., 70–77.
21. Ibid., 54–56.
22. Voss, C. and Raz, T., *Never Split the Difference: Negotiating as if your life depended on it* (New York: HarperCollins Publishers, Inc., 2016), ch. 7.
23. Ibid., 204.

6. *Starting up*

1. Sarasvathy, S.D., *Effectuation – Elements of Entrepreneurial Expertise* (Northampton: Edward Elgar Publishing, Inc., 2008), 81.
2. Cornwell, D., *The Honourable Schoolboy: A George Smiley Novel* (London: Penguin Books, 1977; Kindle edn)
3. https://www.reduser.net/forum/search.php?searchid=42949519
4. Sarasvathy, S.D., *Effectuation – Elements of Entrepreneurial Expertise* (Northampton: Edward Elgar Publishing, Inc., 2008), 34–35.
5. Benioff, M.R., *Behind the Cloud* (San Francisco: Jossey-Bass, 2009), part 1.
6. Segal, G.Z., *Getting There: A Book of Mentors* (New York: Abrams Image, 2015; Kindle edn), 30.
7. Kocienda, K., *Creative Selection* (New York: St. Martin's Press, 2018).
8. https://www.dyson.com/newsroom/overview/features/june-2020/dyson-battery-electric-vehicle.html
9. Ries, E., *The Lean Startup* (London: Portfolio Penguin, 2011), 276.
10. Livingston, J., *Founders at Work* (Berkeley: Apress, 2007), 288.
11. Santos, P.G., *European Founders at Work* (Berkeley: Apress, 2012), 16.
12. https://medium.com/the-mission/the-greatest-sales-deck-ive-ever-seen-4f4ef3391ba0
13. Barwise, P. and Meehan, S., *Simply Better* (Boston: Harvard Business School Publishing, 2004).

14. Sharp, B., *How Brands Grow: What Marketers Don't Know* (South Melbourne: Oxford University Press, 2010), ch. 8.
15. https://www.redbull.com/my-en/energydrink/company-profile
16. https://careers.crocs.com/about-us/default.aspx
17. https://www.youtube.com/watch?v=eywioh_Y5_U
18. http://www.paulgraham.com/think.html
19. Belsky, S., *The Messy Middle* (New York: Portfolio/Penguin, 2018), 195.
20. Ibid., 251.
21. https://techcrunch.com/2013/09/27/why-webvan-failed-and-how-home-delivery-2-0-is-addressing-the-problems/
22. https://www.businessinsider.com/nick-swinmurn-zappos-rnkd-2011-11
23. https://www.inc.com/justin-bariso/amazon-uses-a-secret-process-for-launching-new-ideas-and-it-can-transform-way-you-work.html
24. Vance, A., *Elon Musk: How the Billionaire CEO of SpaceX and Tesla is Shaping our Future* (London: Virgin Digital, 2015), ch. 6.
25. https://www.barrons.com/articles/starlink-spacex-ipo-elon-musk-51624537161

7. Growth

1. For a more comprehensive exploration of this topic, see Raynor, M.E. and Ahmed, M., *The Three Rules: How Exceptional Companies Think* (New York: Portfolio / Penguin, 2013), ch. 4.
2. https://www.wsj.com/articles/uber-co-founder-travis-kalanick-to-depart-companys-board-11577196747
3. I recommend *Confessions of the Pricing Man: How Price Affects Everything* by Hermann Simon, and *The 1% Windfall: How Successful Companies Use Price to Profit and Grow* by Rafi Mohammed as primers on the topic of pricing. *The Strategy and Tactics of Pricing: A Guide to Growing More Profitably* by

Thomas Nagle and John Hogan is a more comprehensive yet challenging read for those wanting to dive deeper.

4. Simon, H., *Confessions of the Pricing Man: How Price Affects Everything* (Switzerland: Springer, 2015; Kindle edn), ch. 3.

5. https://www.nytimes.com/2019/12/18/business/boeing-737-max-suppliers.html

6. Bogomolova, S. and Romaniuk, J., 'Brand defection in a business-to-business financial service' (*Journal of Business Research*, Vol. 62(3, March 2009), 291–296.

7. For a comprehensive explanation of double jeopardy and the other arguments in favour of customer acquisition, see Sharp, B., *How Brands Grow: What Marketers Don't Know* (South Melbourne: Oxford University Press, 2010), and Sharp, B. and Romaniuk, J., *How Brands Grow Part 2* (South Melbourne: Oxford University Press, 2016).

8. https://www.nytimes.com/2020/02/21/business/wells-fargo-settlement.html

9. East, R., Singh, J., Wright, M. and Vanhuele, M., *Consumer Behaviour – Applications in Marketing* (London: Sage Publishing), 35

10. https://www.gartner.com/en/newsroom/press-releases/2021-01-19-gartner-survey-shows-73--of-cmos-will-fall-back-on-lo

11. https://www.usatoday.com/story/money/cars/2018/08/29/best-and-worst-car-brands-of-2018/37633581/

12. 'The reality is that satisfaction is not a predictor of market share. However, market share is a strong negative predictor of future customer satisfaction. So for firms with high market share levels (or goals of attaining high levels), a focus on high satisfaction is not compatible.' See Keiningham, T.L., Aksoy, L., Williams, L. and Buoye, A.J., *The Wallet Allocation Rule: Winning the Battle for Share* (Hoboken, John Wiley & Sons), 13.

13. Byron Sharp and his colleagues at the Ehrenberg-Bass Institute refer to *mental availability* and *physical availability*, although I

prefer the term *buyability* over physical availability, to include a broader spectrum of purchase barriers.

14. I am grateful to evidence-based marketing consultancy The Commercial Works – http://commercialworks.co.uk – for their insights in preparing this section, including the use of their structure: reach, relevance and recognition.

15. Sharp, B. and Romaniuk, J., *How Brands Grow Part 2* (South Melbourne: Oxford University Press, 2016), 41.

16. Romaniuk, J., *Building Distinctive Brand Assets* (South Melbourne: Oxford University Press, 2018), 29.

17. Ibid., ch 4.

18. https://www.thebrandingjournal.com/2015/05/what-to-learn-from-tropicanas-packaging-redesign-failure/

19. https://www.bbc.com/news/business-11520930

20. Sharp, B. and Romaniuk, J., *How Brands Grow Part 2* (South Melbourne: Oxford University Press, 2016), ch. 8.

21. Watkinson, M., *The Grid: The Master Model Behind Business Success* (London: Random House, 2018), 73–82.

22. Keiningham, T.L., Aksoy, L., Williams, L. and Buoye, A.J., *The Wallet Allocation Rule: Winning the Battle for Share* (Hoboken, John Wiley & Sons), ch. 3.

23. I lied about the helicopter fuel, the rest are all real items.

24. Thanks to Luke Williams – co-author of *The Wallet Allocation Rule* – for the critique and additional insight on this topic.

25. *Oakley* (New York: Assouline Publishing, 2014), Heritage.

26. https://blog.aboutamazon.com/company-news/2018-letter-to-shareholders

27. Christensen, C.M., *The Innovator's Solution: Creating and Sustaining Successful Growth* (Boston: Harvard Business Review Press, 2013), ch. 1.

28. https://techcrunch.com/2011/03/31/exclusive-iac-hatches-hatch-a-technology-sandbox-to-incubate-mobile-startups/

29. https://www.theverge.com/2019/5/8/18535869/match-group-tinder-employees-stock-pay-value-lawsuit-payout
30. https://www.pocketgamer.biz/news/68909/monument-valley-worldwide-revenue-climbs-to-over-25-million/
31. https://www.vox.com/2018/1/10/16874054/dominos-ceo-business-stock-price-amazon-facebook-google-pizza
32. https://anyware.dominos.com/
33. https://diginomica.com/domino_digital_100

8. *Lessons for leaders*

1. Management gurus Jim Collins and Jerry Porras advocate for businesses to set Big Hairy Audacious Goals or 'BHAGs'. See Collins, J. and Porras, J., *Built to Last: Successful Habits of Visionary Companies* (New York: Collins Business Essentials, 1994), ch. 5.
2. Burkeman, O., *The Antidote – Happiness for People Who Can't Stand Positive Thinking* (New York: Farrar, Straus and Giroux, 2012), 89.
3. https://www.forbes.com/sites/maggiemcgrath/2016/09/23/the-9-most-important-things-you-need-to-know-about-the-well-fargo-fiasco/?sh=2e61a1893bdc.
4. Martin, R.L., *Fixing the Game* (Boston: Harvard Business School Publishing, 2011), 99.
5. Ibid., 231.
6. Kayes, D.C., *Destructive Goal Pursuit* (New York: Palgrave Macmillan, 2006), 45–49.
7. Oettingen, G., *Rethinking Positive Thinking: Inside the New Science of Motivation* (New York: Current, 2014).
8. Ordóñez, L.D., Schweitzer, M.E., Galinsky, A.D. and Bazerman, M.H., *Goals Gone Wild: The Systematic Side Effects of Over-Prescribing Goal Setting* (Harvard Business School, 2009), 2.
9. Kayes, D.C., *Destructive Goal Pursuit* (New York: Palgrave Macmillan, 2006).

10. Muller, J., *The Tyranny of Metrics* (Princeton: Princeton University Press, 2018), 3.
11. Ibid., 127.
12. Ibid., 171.
13. Gigerenzer, G., *Risk Savvy – How to Make Good Decisions* (New York: Penguin Books, 2014), 44–65.
14. https://www.who.int/news-room/fact-sheets/detail/patient-safety
15. https://www.rolandberger.com/en/Insights/Publications/Decision-making-views-on-risk-and-error-culture.html
16. Dalio, R., *Principles* (New York: Simon & Schuster, 2018), 348.
17. https://rework.withgoogle.com/print/guides/5721312655835136/
18. Clarke, T.R., *The 4 Stages of Psychological Safety* (Oakland: Berrett-Koehler Publishers Inc., 2020), Preface.
19. Holiday, R., *Stillness Is the Key* (New York: Portfolio/Penguin, 2019), 227–229.
20. https://ritzcarltonleadershipcenter.com/2019/03/19/the-power-of-empowerment/
21. Thorndike, W.N., *The Outsiders: Eight Unconventional CEOs and Their Radically Rational Blueprint for Success* (Boston: Harvard Business Review Press, 2012), 191.
22. Page, S.E., *The Difference: How the Power of Diversity Creates Better Groups, Firms, Schools and Societies* (Princeton: Princeton University Press, 2007), 8.
23. Ibid., 162.
24. Ibid., 137.
25. Page, S.E., *The Difference: How the Power of Diversity Creates Better Groups, Firms, Schools and Societies* (Princeton: Princeton University Press, 2007).
26. Sutherland, R., *Alchemy: The Surprising Power of Ideas That Don't Make Sense* (London: WH Allen, 2019), ch. 1.8.
27. Bronowski, J., *The Ascent of Man* (London: BBC Books, 2011), 295.

28. Page, S.E., *The Difference: How the Power of Diversity Creates Better Groups, Firms, Schools and Societies* (Princeton: Princeton University Press, 2007), Preface.

29. https://www.nytimes.com/2021/04/07/opinion/google-job-harassment.html

30. https://twitter.com/ddroga/status/1445530018629971392

31. DeMarco, T., *Slack* (New York: Dorset House, 2001).

32. Goddard, J. and Eccles, T., *Uncommon Sense, Common Nonsense: Why Some Organisations Consistently Outperform Others* (London: Profile Books, 2013), Part One: 'Winners and Losers'.

33. https://web.archive.org/web/20090422100650/http://www.fasterandfaster.net/2008/01/britten-v1000-greatest-motorcycle-ever.html

34. Bahcall, S., *Loonshots: How to Nurture the Crazy Ideas that Win Wars, Cure Diseases, and Transform Industries* (New York: St. Martin's Press, 2019), 12.

35. Ibid., 190–202.

36. Ibid., 149.

37. Ibid., 60–62.

Index

About the Authors

Matt Watkinson is an internationally renowned author, speaker and business consultant. He has been cited and interviewed by the world's leading research firms, and invited to address industry leaders worldwide. His first book, *The Ten Principles Behind Great Customer Experiences*, won the CMI's Management Book of the Year in 2014. His second book, *The Grid: The Master Model Behind Business Success*, appeared in 2017.

Csaba Konkoly was born and raised in Hungary, and launched his first business before turning twenty, importing cars from Italy after the collapse of the Berlin Wall. While studying economics at university, he taught himself to trade stocks, bonds and currencies, and he spent the next seventeen years building and running hedge funds around the world, culminating in a $2+ billion global macro fund. Since then, he has shifted his focus to early-stage tech investments, several of which have become unicorns – valued at over $1 billion each.